PRESENTING AT CONFERENCES, SEMINARS AND MEETINGS

PRESENTING AT CONFERENCES, SEMINARS AND MEETINGS

Kerry Shephard

SAGE Publications
London • Thousand Oaks • New Delhi

SAGE Publications Ltd
1 Oliver's Yard
55 City Road
London EC1Y 1SP

SAGE Publications Inc.
2455 Teller Road
Thousand Oaks, California 91320

SAGE Publications India Pvt Ltd
B-42, Panchsheel Enclave
Post Box 4109
New Delhi 110 017

British Library Cataloguing in Publication data

A catalogue record for this book is available
from the British Library

ISBN 1 4129 0342 4
ISBN 1 4129 0343 2 (pbk)

Library of Congress Control Number: 2004094665

Typeset by C&M Digitals (P) Ltd., Chennai, India
Printed in Great Britain by TJ International, Padstow, Cornwall

Contents

Preface

Who and what is this book for?

This book is intended for lecturers and researchers at universities and colleges heading off to an academic conference and for teachers and other professionals presenting papers or contributing in other ways, for example, to the annual meeting of their professional body. It will be relevant to undergraduate and postgraduate students preparing for their project presentation and for visiting academics preparing for important departmental seminars. The key elements of these situations are that the speaker or presenter is expected to be knowledgeable and enthusiastic about her or his topic and to be able to communicate information clearly. To some extent the speaker attempts to encourage the audience to learn about something – although the speaker is not there to teach in a conventional way. The speaker also attempts to motivate, even persuade, the audience – although the speaker would always deny that he or she is there to sell anything. So this book is designed to help professional people undertake an important part of their professional role: to present at conferences, seminars and meetings.

This book addresses key aspects of presenting in a variety of settings, including videoconferencing and the web-cast, the use of audio-visual aids of many kinds, how to avoid disasters and what to do when disasters occur. I make no excuses for the inclusion of 'technology'. Many books avoid the difficult elements of technology-supported presentation even though, in most academic settings, technology makes an important contribution. Some would prefer this not to be the case. Some might wish that PowerPoint, video projectors and the Internet had never arisen. But there they are, at every conference, waiting to engage, or bore, us. We may choose not to use technology to support our presentations but we should not ignore what it has to offer. Our choice should be based on knowledge and experience, not anxiety or fear.

It is also important to say what the book is *not* about. It is neither about lecturing, nor about public speaking in a general sense. The first suggests more sustained 'learner-support' and the second often implies a focus on 'entertainment'. Nor is it about the broader conference experience, although I do accept that such a book would be useful for many. It will not, sadly, help readers get their papers accepted for the conference programme or prepare conference goers for the social demands of the experience. I wish that I did have demonstrable expertise to share in these areas, but I do not think that I do.

How to use this book

For many this book will not be a 'cover-to-cover' read. I hope that the index will be useful, and that the introductory paragraphs in each chapter will guide you to the bits that you need. If you have a presentation to give next week, turn straight to Chapter 8. If your presentation is via a video link, then Chapter 7 should help. Both of these chapters are designed to be relatively self-contained. If you have longer to prepare yourself, Chapter 1 attempts to identify the attributes of good presentation that many of us aspire to. Chapter 3 looks at presentation aids and technologies. Chapter 4 is about designing your presentation; Chapter 5 focuses on you, the presenter; and Chapter 6 looks at things from the perspective of the organizers of your conference, seminar or meeting. Chapter 9 explores longer-term self-development. All of this is supported by Chapter 2's assessment of the theoretical underpinning of presenting at conferences, seminars and meetings.

For those entirely new to presenting at conferences, seminars and meetings, a short advice-box is included at the end of the first seven chapters. However, I do hope that new presenters will read more than these boxes!

I should also comment on my writing style. I have made a conscious effort to write informally; a style very different from my normal academic writing. I hope that this makes the book readable and therefore more usable. I have tried to re-create the spoken style that I adopt in an academic development setting. To this end, I also made use of speech recognition software to enable me to dictate, rather than type, some of the text. Much of the content in this book relates closely to the content of my professional development workshops so the words were not new to me. I enjoyed writing in this way but I had to be careful to avoid rewriting it in a more formal style whilst editing it!

What can I contribute? What makes me qualified to write this book?

Before I buy a 'how to do it book' I need to know what makes the author think that she or he has something worth saying. I would expect a book about cooking to be written by an author with considerably more culinary skills than I possess. Perhaps I would expect the author to be an expert cook? Well, I have never considered myself to be an expert conference presenter (some of my presentations have been dismal), but due to a range of particular circumstances I think that, probably, I know enough about conference presentations to claim 'expert' knowledge about them. Having said that, I hasten to add that this book is more than a review of the literature!

My background

I gave my first ever 'presentation' as a third-year undergraduate. I was very nervous. All my peers were there along with several senior staff from the department. I had no idea how it would go. I had never seen myself 'on video'. I had never even heard a tape-recording of my voice. I had literally no idea about how others perceived me. I have always been shy. I had done some preparation (I did have notes) but I did not know if it would be enough. I had no real audio-visual aids although I do remember drawing a picture of a lost turtle on the board. I have a poor memory and discovered early on that I was quite incapable of learning any substantial text word for word. The occasion promised to be a total disaster for me and my career.

It was not, in the event, a disaster. I discovered that words did come out in approximately the right order. Most importantly, I discovered that people listened to me. I remember vividly that I seemed able to engage the attention of the audiences and my surprise that my peers thought that I was saying something worth listening to. This event boosted my confidence.

This new-found confidence supported my subsequent career as a lecturer and researcher in biology. Over a period of 25 years I lectured to thousands of students and presented at dozens of conferences, seminars and meetings. I experienced the very best and worst of presentations on a regular basis but it was not until later that I developed an interest in the processes of presentation and sought a theoretical underpinning. I developed an interest in innovative approaches to teaching that gradually absorbed my research time. My career switched to educational and staff development and I found myself supporting the development of staff in higher education.

My workshops

One of the commonest development aims of staff in higher education, particularly those that work in research-led institutions, is to improve their conference presentations. For the past few years I have run workshops where small groups of academic staff and postgraduate students reflect on their own presentation styles and provide supportive feedback to others in the group. Participants from all disciplines describe their own views on what makes a good presentation and what constraints their own subject area places on how they present. For my part, I work hard to enable participants to give and receive useful feedback and to depart with their confidence boosted. In return I receive the benefit of greater knowledge and understanding of participants' views on what makes a good presentation and how presentations can be improved. I intend to build on much of this throughout this book.

What is in the public domain?

I said earlier that this book is more than just a review of the literature, but it does include elements of the literature. Presenting is not totally a-theoretical. In addition there is much in the education and educational psychology literature that is relevant, in that it does examine the evidence that supports or negates the paradigms of presenting. Academic readers, in particular, should not ignore the benefits of academic endeavour, but nor should we suspend judgement on their application.

Common sense

I will also make a point of using common sense to distinguish between useful advice and unnecessary detail. Participants on my workshops generally manage to describe elements of good presentation without reference to Aristotle, ERIC or social constructivism. For them, a presenter who looks at her notes all of the time is not as engaging as one who looks at the audience for at least some of the time. Actually there is an underpinning theory here and also some supporting experimental evidence. And is this really common sense or could it be the collective experience of the professions passed on to students through many years of education? So when does the detail become unnecessary? At what point does good common sense become dogma? What needs to be supported by evidence and what can be taken for granted? Read on!

What will readers gain from reading this book?

There are two elements to this question.

What are the benefits of successful presentation?

From my experience, going to a conference or seminar and giving a poor presentation is a little like writing a research grant application and then putting it in the bin instead of in the mail. It will do you no good and may do you a lot of harm. Unless you have enormous stores of resilience, resourcefulness or gumption, it will make you feel really bad about yourself. But, giving a good presentation will boost your confidence and make you feel good about yourself. You will return invigorated and refreshed.

From the viewpoint of participants on my workshops, most participants would not have put it that way but nor would they, I think, disagree. Conferences and seminars are important career-building events.

From the academic literature, I know of no studies that have explored the measurable benefits – to career and well-being – of successful conference and seminar presentation. How could something so important be missed by academic enquiry?

Will this book help you to present at conferences, seminars and meetings?

I hope that this book will help you. It is designed to act as a change agent and work in partnership with you, as a reader and presenter, to improve your presentations. Please give me some feedback; balanced if possible, good and bad.

Kerry Shephard

Acknowledgements

I would like to acknowledge the support and encouragement of colleagues in the Centre for Learning and Teaching at the University of Southampton and the input of 'critical friends' and reviewers. I must also acknowledge the contribution of all of those academic staff and students whose presentations I have attended, enjoyed and learned from.

1

What Makes Some Presentations Good?

Key concepts in this chapter:

■ Types of presentations.

■ What do you think contributes to good presentation?

■ What others think contributes to good presentation.

■ Five categories to work with.

■ Content, structure, self-presentation, interaction and presentation aids.

■ Subject- and place-differences in expectations.

■ Some people appear to break all of the rules.

■ What contributes to bad presentations?

This chapter encourages us to think about what makes presentations good, and then follows this with an analysis of what many others have suggested. The chapter will also consider what tends to be viewed as bad presentation and what most often goes wrong in presentations. Three case studies and additional content will illustrate how the subject, venue and circumstances influence acceptable practice. A central aim of this chapter is to demystify the essential elements of what makes some presentations good, particularly to encourage those new to presenting. Most people agree on what makes presentations good and the characteristics of good presentations are not particularly surprising. Good content, understandable structure, interactions between presenter and audience, reasonable self-presentation and helpful use of presentation aids are all elements of good practice. There are subject differences in expectation, but new presenters should be able to research what is acceptable in their own discipline. It is rare for presenters to do everything 'right' and there is a lot of scope for individual self-expression.

As we explore the characteristics of good presentations, we should also have in our minds the range of possible presentations. New presenters are often asked to undertake research project presentations as their first experience, either individually or in small groups. At a later stage in their career they may give a departmental seminar or a short conference presentation. Alternatively they may prepare for a poster presentation. Most researchers find themselves contributing to a research group presentation at some stage. More experienced professionals will be thinking about contributing to a panel presentation or to a symposium. Researchers at the peak of their career may be enticed to offer a keynote presentation to a large international conference. Although the range is significant all of these presentation-types have much in common.

Brainstorming the issues: what makes presentations good?

Let's start with your views on what makes a good presentation. I do not think that it would be possible, or desirable, to impose a fixed external model of a good presentation on to everyone. For one thing, it would not work as it ignores our own individual strengths and weaknesses that we really do need to address. For another, it would result, if successful, in very dull conferences and meetings! So, let's start with your views.

> Think about the last really good presentation that you went to: a lecture, a conference presentation, a sales pitch or, as a last resort, a television presentation. Write down six things that you thought were good about the presentation.

Use a blank piece of paper for this. You need to keep the list for future reference. If possible, please do this task before you read on or look at the figures in this chapter.

What others say

Common responses

When I facilitate staff development workshops on 'Presenting your Research at Conferences' I ask participants to do this task before attending the workshop.

I am confident that generally they do. I also use the task as an initial activity for pairs of participants in the early stages of the workshop. Participants at this stage are still apprehensive about the workshop. They do not know other participants and it is important that they rapidly feel at ease with them and with me. They need an activity that they feel comfortable with, that they can contribute to and will make them feel that they have something in common with other participants. If the task produced too many differences it would not work in this way. If each participant identified particular aspects of a presentation that were good for them but not for others, then this initial group activity would be more divisive than community-building. So here is the point: **Generally people from academic backgrounds, from all subject areas that I have experience of, have common views on what makes presentations good.** This applies to experienced academics and young postgraduate students alike. Of course there are individual differences and subject differences and I will describe these later. Naturally much of the detail emerges with differences of opinion, later; but generally people agree on a whole range of key issues. As I watch and listen to pairs or small groups of participants describe their experiences of good presentations I see and hear the surprise and relief that their views are commonly held views and that they do have things in common with other participants. It is at this stage that I see people relax into the workshop and start to really get involved.

Within the workshop I usually record the views of individuals and small groups on a flip chart. I ask each pair to identify one aspect of a presentation that they think is good. Sometimes individuals within the pair modify the phrase used by the spokesperson, but generally members of the pair reach a consensus on the statement. We then briefly discuss the statement in the wider group and it is unusual for the statement to be radically different from that on the lists of all other pairs. Then I ask another group to identify another aspect, and so on. A typical flip chart, after this activity, looks something like Figure 1.1 (this is not a reproduction from any particular workshop but a synthesis from many).

There follows a period of comparison, regrouping and consolidation. Some statements turn out to be quite similar to others and can be combined. Most importantly we try to group statements so as to reduce the number of variables that we will work on in the remaining workshop. Subdivision in this way is useful if it identifies clear elements of our own practice that we can work on to improve. It is clear from Figure 1.1 that some statements are about the presentation itself (e.g. 'The presentation had a logical structure'), while others

FIGURE 1.1

A typical flip chart record of workshop participants' views on what aspect of a presentation they think as good.

Uses good examples		Good timing
Its level was right for the audience	The presentation had a logical structure	The central ideas were summarized at the end
Appropriate use of data	I could take useful notes	I knew where the presentation was going
To the point; not much waffle	She looked at the audience	She knew her subject well
		Did not read from a script
He handled the questions well	It seemed honest	He asked the audience some questions and got answers
	Fluent speaker	
She had a professional appearance	Good use of English	She had charisma
He engaged with the audience from the start	She looked relaxed	The slides were clear and useful
She spoke to the audience	She was enthusiastic	He did not just read his PowerPoint bullet points

are more about the presenter (e.g. 'She looked at the audience'). This is one useful subdivision. Perhaps you can look at your own list and decide how easy it would be to apply this subdivision.

There are other fairly natural divisions. In relation to the presentation, it is useful to separate its structure from its content. Indeed, in Chapter 4, this is an important design feature that we will examine in depth. One other division is possibly less intuitive but I think that it provides a sound basis for further analysis and improvement. In relation to the presenter, rather than the presentation, I think that it is useful to divide aspects of how the presenter interacts with the audience from how the presenter 'presents' her- or himself.

This analysis gives us four major subdivisions: Structure, Content, Interaction and Self-Presentation. In my experience of many workshops, dividing the statements of what makes presentations good into these four categories proves to be relatively easy and occurs without controversy.

There is one other category that is important to us, and groups differ in how they want to work with it. Many presentations, but certainly not all, make substantial use of audio-visual or presentation aids. Workshop participants have suggested almost universally that the way the presenter works with audio-visual aids is a substantial factor in deciding whether a presentation is good or bad; but the precise details of what is good or bad practice in their use varies considerably. It is arguable that presentation aids and their use actually form part of the content of a presentation, influence and describe its structure, provide a mechanism for interacting with the audience and provide a platform for the presenter's self-presentation. On this basis no separate category for the use of audio-visual aids is needed. I sometimes make this argument but invariably lose it. The workshop participants value the adoption of a separate category for presentation aids, so we shall maintain it here and discuss the issue further; both below and in Chapter 3.

Figure 1.2 provides my attempt to categorize the statements provided in Figure 1.1. Can you undertake the same categorization of your statements? Do you have a list that includes completely different statements? Do you have views about what makes a good presentation that are similar to the views of others or are your views different?

Odd responses?

There will always be a variety of views. Academic staff at universities and colleges are perhaps a particularly diverse group, drawn together only by a common desire to research and teach, and often with very little else in common. There is no reason why everyone in this group should hold the same views on presentation style and every reason why there should be some individuals with different views.

What surprises me most, however, is that it is very rare for individuals to have markedly different views at this stage. Participants may feel that they personally cannot achieve the standards expressed in the group activity and this may influence their expression of their views. I have also encountered individuals who feel unable to say what they think makes a good presentation, but who are perfectly able to express what makes a bad presentation. There is presumably some individual-difference psychology here that I am not experienced in interpreting (but I do have my own ideas about this!).

Perhaps your statements, about what makes a presentation good, are particularly different from those provided in Figure 1.1. Is that a problem? Figure 1.1 represents the best combination of preferences that I can generate, based on the views of numerous workshop participants over several years. They are also fairly self-evident. Generally speaking, no one would expect a

FIGURE 1.2

The same record as in Figure 1.1 but here categorized as views on content, structure, self-presentation, interaction and presentation aids.

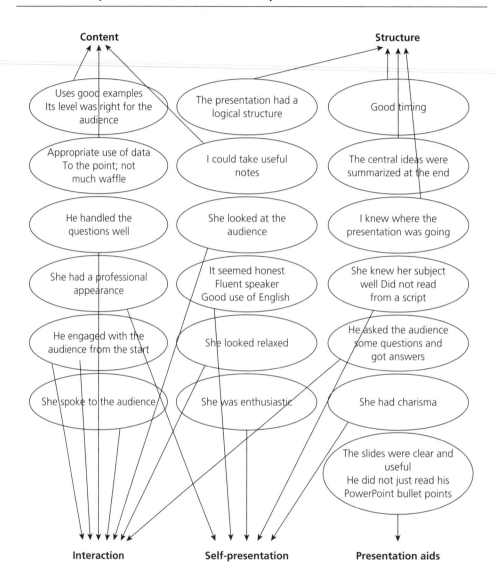

presentation lacking in structure to be particularly good, or a presenter who uses no examples of relevance to the audience to be particularly engaging. Most of this is fairly down-to-earth. But then consider the experiences of most academics. They attend lectures, conferences and seminars, mostly in their own subject areas and mostly given by people that they know. Does this fit with your own experience? Add to this the fact that, for most of us, many presentations that we attend are 'not that good'. Very few would ever exemplify all of the positive attributes listed in Figure 1.1. If we are lucky, some of them would display some of these positive attributes. Figure 1.1 is therefore a wish-list, synthesized from the wishes of many, rather than an expectation. Your wish-list might be different from Figure 1.1, but that does not make it less desirable for you.

There is another factor. Most of the key statements in Figure 1.1 are rather broad. 'She knew her subject well' is not particularly precise. It represents an impression given by the presenter to the audience. It could have been achieved in a variety of ways; some of which may have been illusory, rather than real. The statement provides a broad aim but not enough detail to enable us to determine how this particular feat was done. Hidden in this breadth could have been any number of precise statements. Perhaps your statements do not match those in Figure 1.1 because you chose to address the issue at a different level.

For now we must address the five key considerations described in Figure 1.2

Some conclusions: five key considerations

For much of the rest of this book we will work with five categories of statements about what makes presentations good. These are now described.

Content

This is the core of what is said in a presentation and in many respects the easiest thing for a presenter to change or adapt. Audiences tend to appreciate content that matches the presentation's title and delivered at a pace and level to suit the audience.

Structure

Audiences acknowledge that structures can take many forms but generally they appreciate some indication of the major subdivisions of the presentation and other details such as how long it is likely to last and whether, or not, questions and answers form part of the presenter's plans.

Self-presentation

Audiences like honest presenters, or at least presenters who appear to be honest. They also tend to like enthusiastic presenters but to dislike over-enthusiastic presenters. Most importantly they appreciate presenters who appear to know what they are talking about. Much of this depends on how audiences interpret what they see or hear.

Interaction

Most audiences want to feel as if the presenter has noticed that they are there. A presenter who talks to a whiteboard and fails to look at people in the audience is generally not appreciated.

Audio-visuals or presentation aids

For presentations that make use of audio-visual aids this often is the 'big one'. Well-used aids can contribute positively to all four categories above. Badly-used aids generally just get labelled as badly-used.

Subject differences, place differences and humour

Consider the following statement:

> Everyone knows that academics tend to display tribal characteristics. The tribes relate most strongly to the subject or discipline. Of course we should avoid stereotyping this diverse profession but aspects of clothing, speech and body language do often indicate whether the professor in front of us specializes in modern history, business studies or computer science.

Actually, in my experience, this is nonsense. Certainly if I had to guess someone's academic subject from their clothing, speech or body language, I think I would fail dismally. People in academia are just too diverse for this. However, I would have a better chance if I saw their presentation style. Despite what is recorded above about academics' (from all subjects) views on what makes presentations good, when it actually comes to presenting there are subject differences. It is almost as if people have their own views on what makes the best presentations but that their discipline imposes constraints on how they actually present.

One of the clearest expressions of this is how acceptable it is for a presenter to read from a script. Almost universally, academic staff tell me that the appearance of spontaneous speaking makes for a better presentation than reading from a script. But many academic staff from the humanities then go on to tell me that this is fine for others, but for them, in their subject setting, at their particular conferences, seminars and meetings, they will be expected to prepare a script, to have it in front of them and to stick to it. Some go so far as to say that they are expected to remember it verbatim, so that they can speak to the audience without appearing to read the script. These academic staff tell me that the words in their presentation have to be carefully crafted and that there is no room for improvisation. Given that a script is necessary, they either have to learn it word for word or they must read from the script. Most of these presenters probably do something in between. The consequences of this imperative, along with other subject-related design factors, will be addressed in Chapter 4.

How people perceive the good and bad in presentations is also greatly dependent on factors that relate to place and related circumstances. Presentations can easily be viewed as too formal or too informal, depending on where they are given and the circumstances. Keynote presentations are expected to provide something different from the run of the mill presentations that follow. Presentations for a departmental seminar are generally longer and less formal than those for a major international conference. But how can you judge just what will be appropriate and what will not? The key here is really to anticipate what the audience expects, or will cope with, and this requires a degree of audience-research.

Humour is perhaps the toughest of all attributes to identify as good or bad. Participants on my workshops give mixed messages here. Some like humour in a presentation and some do not. Figure 1.1 does not include a reference to humour; although many individuals include it on their lists of good aspects of presentations, many do not and have voiced opposition to its inclusion. I have not found a particular correlation to subject, gender or age here. Readers of this book will know that there are other sources of guidance for presenting at conferences, seminars and meetings (some of them are listed in the Bibliography). Many of these recommend the use of humour in presentations. Lenn Millbower, as one of many proponents, has written an article for Presenter's

University, a website devoted to presentation skills. Lenn's article, 'Laugh and learn', suggests that:

> **Laughter is an important component in any presentation. Even when (the) presenter ignores humor, the attendees find it, sometimes at the presenter's expense. The need for laughter is so strong that participants seek out opportunities to laugh throughout every seminar. They do so with good reason. It is natural and appropriate to use humor in learning situations. It is, for a number of reasons, also demonstrative of solid instructional design. (Millbower, 2003)**

The article is persuasive and I do agree with much of it, but I still have reservations. Perhaps the issue is primarily about audience expectations. Generally, I like to make people laugh in informal presentations, for example at departmental seminars, because at heart I do agree with much of what Lenn Millbower says. (Naturally, I want them to laugh with me, not at me.) But I tend not to attempt to make people laugh in formal presentations, for example, at major conferences. Partly this is because I am not brave enough; partly it is because I do not know the audience well enough to be sure about what will be seen as humorous and what will not; but mostly it is because participants at the important conferences that I go to do not expect me to be funny. They might expect other, better known, presenters to be funny, but not me. Perhaps I need to practise being humorous more. Perhaps we all do, so that humour becomes more universally acceptable at conferences. But in the meantime, humour remains a highly personal aspect of good or bad presentations.

Many of these issues will re-emerge in later chapters.

Three case studies

These three case studies consider near extremes in presentation style and they are included to encourage readers to consider alternative views on what makes presentations good.

Not all lecturers display characteristics of the 'absent-minded professor' but some do and there does appear to be room in academic settings for amiable, avuncular but (apparently) poorly organized presenters. Cast your mind back to your last conference. Did you spot one? Maybe you even have one in your department? What are their characteristics? Perhaps a shoelace is frequently undone. Perhaps their hair is untidy, their tie has a stain on it or is even tucked into their trousers? Perhaps they approach the podium with an armful of unruly papers, stumbling on the way. Do they have a wild look in their eyes? Do they carry an overflowing handbag? Do they have a spelling problem? But do they always have some interesting things to say, possibly said with humour? Do they give the sort of presentation that you remember? Are they, perhaps, actually, good presenters in an odd sort of way? Not that you would want to mimic them of course, but let's not be too dismissive of variety (Case study 1.1).

At the other extreme we should consider the outright professional. Is there still a place for the presenter who presents in the same way as they (allegedly) did in the Royal Institution in 1900? In my own subject areas I think that presentations like this are the exception rather than the rule, but this is not necessarily so in other subject areas. I know that colleagues in history and English departments often do still admire, perhaps even expect, this level of professionalism. In some respects we aim for the *appearance* of this professionalism in a range of other settings. Broadcasters, for example, often give extraordinarily good presentations (with the illusion of spontaneity and the precision of the prepared text) but they also benefit from the autocue, direction, rehearsals and retakes (Case study 1.2).

The notion of careful use of presentation aids is then considered in our third case as we experience a struggling undergraduate student who produced a presentation that impressed her peers (Case study 1.3).

CASE STUDY 1.1
The disorganized lecturer

Simon carried an armful of papers and overhead transparencies to the podium, thanking the Chairman on the way. He spent some time sorting out his aids and testing the overhead projector (OHP) before he looked at the audience and introduced his presentation. He had no notes in front of him and there was no indication that his presentation was remembered word for word; sentences seemed to be lacking in some aspects of grammar and there were quite a few ers and ums as Simon thought about how to express particular concepts. The introduction seemed to lack organization, some important aspects were given as if an afterthought, but I was in no doubt about where the presentation was going and what I was expected to get out of it. He moved to the OHP quite quickly after his introduction and placed a transparency on it. He turned to check that the slide was in focus and that it could be seen, but did not appear to notice that it was not straight with respect to the screen. While Simon spoke about aspects of the figure he pointed sometimes to the figure on the OHP with his finger and sometimes to the projected image, again with his finger (either he had not noticed that a laser pointer had been provided or he had decided not to use it). He looked everywhere, and at everyone, but also took some time out to look at his figures as if he was trying to interpret them himself, there and then. As he did so he spoke his thoughts out aloud, debating the possible interpretations himself. He had quite a few figures to show us and certainly some were just flashed before our eyes while others were quite possibly lost in the pile. They were not really necessary, he explained. Simon ran out of time and the Chairman had to stand to indicate that it was time to move on. This seemed to prompt Simon, not to leave, but to summarize his presentation. This he did with clarity in perhaps 30 seconds. He left us with a list of questions that were to form the basis of his research, and perhaps that of others, until the next conference.

This presentation probably does not conform to many of the statements of what makes presentations good, listed in Figure 1.1. In relation to our five key considerations, a 'critical friend' might make the following observations:

Content: of significant interest to the audience and at about the right level.
Structure: appeared to lack structure but all of the intended outcomes described early on were achieved.
Self-presentation: unorthodox but clearly enthusiastic and committed.
Interaction: useful examples, good eye contact, engaging – we were left with some interesting questions to think about.
Presentation aids: unorthodox, tending to sloppy, but some visual aids were completely integrated into the presentation.

Was it a bad presentation? I think that, actually, it was a good presentation. I had seen Simon present before so I knew his style. I knew what Simon was going to talk about from the first few minutes. I felt engaged by the presentation and I enjoyed being part of his apparent exploration of the issues. I remember aspects of this presentation far more than any other in that conference. I would not try to mimic it because I know that I could not; nor would I advise others to use Simon as their role model.

If you think that this is 'you' then I do advise you to seek feedback from trusted colleagues. When the comedian Jimmy Tarbuck was interviewed on the radio programme *Desert Island Discs,* he said that veteran comedian Eric Morecambe had once given Jimmy some feedback on his highly individual style as a comic. Eric apparently commented that Jimmy had something special and he recommended that Jimmy should never attempt to analyse it. I might offer the same advice to Simon, if I were asked, but I suspect that Simon already has confidence in his ability to present, his way.

CASE STUDY 1.2
The organized professional

James was the outgoing President of a learned society. His duty was to present the Presidential Address at the Society's annual conference in a neighbouring country. Preparing this presentation was his preoccupation for months before the conference. James had also been the Chairman of the academic department in which I was a postdoctoral research fellow. I saw the work that he put into his presentation. I saw the 'lights on late' in the department's lecture theatre. I heard small samples of the presentation being practised and revised as I walked past his door. I was also giving a presentation at the conference but I must admit that I did nowhere near as much preparation.

Near the end of the conference, everyone gathered in the largest lecture room available. The audience was hushed. James was introduced by the conference convener and he walked to the lectern. James was dressed impeccably. He looked at ease and in command. He had a typed script in his hand but laid this firmly on the lectern. He knew exactly where the controls for the lights and audio-visual aids were and he used them faultlessly. Clearly he had practised in this room as well as in our lecture theatre at home. James spoke fluently to everyone in the room. I noticed that he looked at me for a time before he turned his attention to others in the room. His presentation was on his own research topic but was designed to be of interest to a wide range of listeners. There was something in it for just about everyone, including a number of well-chosen examples to enable lay-members of the audience to stay involved. He used well-chosen slides to illustrate points and avoided the use of technical terms. Where these were necessary he defined them and illustrated their use with the slides. James used a pointer to identify important areas of his slides. James had provided an introduction to his presentation so that we could follow its structure as it took place. The conference programme had also provided clear times for its start and finish. It started on time. It also finished on time; exactly. Clearly much of James's preparations had involved practice to ensure that the presentation finished on time. I think that it was memorized, word for word.

The audience applauded. They knew that they had experienced a professional academic's professional presentation. It might not have been the presentation that everyone would have given (there was, for example, no humour in it and I doubt that many in the audience would have been capable of such faultless timing) but I am confident that everyone in the room admired its professionalism.

In my own subject areas I think that presentations like this are rare exceptions; but this is not so in other subject areas. In relation to our five key considerations, another 'critical friend' might make the following observations:

Content: perfect for the occasion and delivered at a level appropriate to the full range of delegates.

Structure: impeccable; easily understood by all in the audience.

Self-presentation: totally professional.

Interaction: good examples, good eye contact, possibly a little 'remote' but perfect for the occasion.

Presentation aids: high quality visual aids used to illustrate points very well.

CASE STUDY 1.3
The undergraduate project presentation

Clare was very worried about her project presentation and I was not surprised. She had not actually done as much work on her project as I had hoped. (She led a very active social life alongside her third-year undergraduate studies.) Nor was Clare a high-achiever in her academic assessments. She was, however, not shy. She could hold her own in any conversation or group activity. The presentation was not graded but it was compulsory. I think that Clare had anticipated her likely problems well. She thought that she would stand up in front of the group and forget what to say in exactly the same way that she forgets what to write in an examination. She admitted that she was not particularly interested in her project topic but didn't think that was the real problem. Even if she were asked to talk about her favourite pop group she would still find it difficult to maintain a structured presentation. The important points just didn't come to her mind at the right time. Clare knew that she could read from a script but also that she would be disappointed in herself if she resorted to this again. She wanted desperately to be congratulated by her peers for presenting well.

I suggested that she tried to use PowerPoint to add structure, and key information, to her presentation. This was in the mid-1990s. PowerPoint was not widely used for undergraduate presentations at that time and we did struggle to get everything set up. (The facility was then offered to other students, several of whom did adopt it.) Clare initially agreed to use PowerPoint to prepare overhead transparencies, but after working with the software for a day or so, felt prepared to use PowerPoint itself to deliver the slides. She was glad that she did. The presentation worked wonderfully for her. Clare's natural confidence and ability to 'chat' around any topic was exactly complemented by PowerPoint's delivery of Clare's crisp bullet points and structure. Clare's peers were absolutely amazed, but I wasn't. With the right tools that girl could go far.

An important point here is that of anticipation. Clare and I knew what her problems were likely to be and found a tool that enabled her to gain maximum credit for her strengths while having her weaknesses supported. In relation to our five key considerations, Clare's 'critical friend' might make the following observations:

Content: of interest to the audience and at about the right level. We had heard about Clare's project in part, but it was good to see it all come together here.
Structure: clear structure, clearly presented using PowerPoint.
Self-presentation: Clare looked so confident and really spoke well about her project. We had no idea that she had taken it so seriously. She seems to know lots and did make it clear when there were areas that she did not cover in her project.
Interaction: Clare spoke to everyone in the audience as if we were her best friends. It was more like a chat about the topic than a formal presentation, but that got us all involved.
Presentation aids: Clare's slides were to the point. Perhaps some of the text was not necessary but it clearly helped Clare to keep on track.

What makes some presentations bad?

This question paraphrases one that will be considered in depth in Chapter 8, what tends to go wrong? It is also possible to reverse most of the statements in Figure 1.1 to list aspects of presentations that most people consider to be bad. The list in Table 1.1 attempts to combine these two concepts by relating what most often goes wrong to characteristics of presentations most often considered to be undesirable. With the exception of arriving late at the conference or

TABLE 1.1

This table describes aspects of presentations that often fail and relates these to commonly reported views on what makes presentations good and bad.

WHAT TENDS TO GO WRONG	WHAT MAKES PRESENTATIONS GOOD	WHAT MAKES PRESENTATIONS BAD
Lack of content	Its level was right for the audience I could take useful notes To the point; not much waffle She knew her subject well	Level was wrong for the audience Audience cannot take notes Waffle Not knowing your subject well
Boring content	Did not read from a script She was enthusiastic She had charisma	Reading from a script Lacking enthusiasm Lacking charisma
Timing	Good timing	Poor timing
You lose the audience	The presentation had a logical structure The central ideas were summarized at the end I knew where the presentation was going	Lack of a logical structure Not providing a summary at the end Not identifying where the presentation is going at the start
Nerves	She looked relaxed Good use of English Fluent speaker	Not looking relaxed Not using good English or speaking fluently
Is it believable?	Appropriate use of data It seemed honest She had a professional appearance	Inappropriate use of data Appearing to be dishonest Having an unprofessional appearance
Inability to interact with the audience	Uses good examples She looked at the audience He engaged with the audience from the start She spoke to the audience	Not using good examples Not looking at the audience Not engaging with the audience from the start Not speaking to the audience
Questions and answers	He handled the questions well He asked the audience some questions and got answers	Handling questions badly Asking the audience some questions but not getting answers
Technology	He did not just read his PowerPoint bullet points The slides were clear and useful	Just reading your PowerPoint bullet points Slides neither clear nor useful

meeting, this table does illustrate most of the attributes of presentations that academic staff and postgraduate students most often express as poor.

Summary

I hope that sections in this chapter illustrate that there are few strict rules in presentation. In general, not everyone will agree with generalizations all of the time. But Table 1.1 does give a reasonable guide to what most of us need to do, most of the time, to deliver good presentations. As we shall see, some things are easier to achieve than others!

Reference

Millbower, L. (2003) 'Laugh and Learn'. Presenter's University http://www.presenters university.com/courses_content_laugh.php (accessed 7 January 2003).

Encouragement for new presenters

Those new to presenting should take heart from the contents of this chapter.

- Most people agree on what makes presentations good.
- The characteristics of good presentations are not surprising: good content, understandable structure, interactions between presenter and audience, reasonable self-presentation and helpful use of presentation aids.
- There are subject differences in expectation, but you should be able to research what is acceptable in your subject.
- It is rare for a presenter to do everything 'right' and your own experience demonstrates that some presentations are very poor. You can do better than that. Much better.

This book aims to help you overcome your weaknesses and build on your strengths.

2

What Do We Really Know About Presenting?

Key concepts in this chapter:

■ Searching for a theoretical underpinning to presenting.

■ Contributions from social psychology, business studies and education.

■ What do conferences, seminars and meetings contribute?

■ Your contribution to the social construction of knowledge.

■ Why an e-mail might not be as good as a presentation.

■ Can you learn good presentation skills and can they be taught?

Chapter 1 describes what people think and feel contributes to good presentation. This, however, may not be enough for academic and other professional readers of this book. These readers will wish to identify the building blocks for presentation, in the same way as they might look for the those of accountancy or law. In relation to presentation skills, our task is to identify what exactly we are learning, what is known about it, and what is not, where this knowledge comes from and how sure we are about it. Only then will we want to learn these skills and to put this learning into practice. Whether you are an experienced academic researcher, a postgraduate student or an undergraduate preparing for your first project presentation, I think that you should question what we think we know about presentation.

Does presentation have a theoretical underpinning and a literature?

Chapter 1 presents a case for describing presentations in terms of five main descriptors: content, structure, self-presentation and interaction, plus the use of presentation aids. This classification is based entirely on the views of academic staff asked to reflect on good presentation style. These variables are not themselves theoretically based, nor are they the hypothesis or invention of any particular academic guru. They are elements of a convenient classification that stem from the personal experiences and reflections of many. But it is always a pleasure to compare such descriptors to key parameters in the traditional field of rhetoric (the study of effective speaking and writing). Aristotle, more than two thousand years ago, used the terms pathos, ethos and logos. I do not, myself, think that these terms, or the five canons of rhetoric (invention, arrangement, style, memory and delivery) relate to a particular and fundamental law that defines what is good and bad about a presentation. It would be difficult, for example, to create a predictive and quantifiable model from them. But the concepts are useful. They relate well to personal experience and they carry the weight of a substantial field of human endeavour.

Logos is the propositional content of what is said. It is the factual content of a presentation without reference to how it is communicated. The 'how' comes in the form of ethos and pathos. Ethos relates most strongly to who is giving the presentation. The same content, delivered by different speakers may well have different impacts on an audience. Self-presentation is all-important here: 'There is something about this speaker that makes me want to listen.' Pathos also describes aspects of how a presentation is given. Pathos relates to the emotional response that the content, and the presenter, engender in the audience. The structure of a presentation is important here, to help the audience understand and follow the argument. Interaction between presenter and audience is most significant. Enthusiasm, passion and emotional engagement with the audience (perhaps by the use of carefully selected examples), can enable some presenters, in some circumstances, to deliver a good presentation.

Modern theories?

So, have we learned more about presentation in the past two thousand years? There is, in fact, no shortage of modern day theories of communication that have a bearing on presenting at conferences, seminars and meetings. The field of rhetoric has continued to expand, along with that of oratory (the art of public speaking). The scientific and social scientific disciplines of education and psychology have contributed much; as indeed has the relatively new field of business studies. The starting points may be different, depending on a desire to teach, to support learning, to understand or to sell; but the contributions are probably all valid.

I like the theories of F.E.X. Dance. I will expand on his ideas on speech, thought and critical thinking later in this chapter but here I need to describe his ideas on oratory. Dance (1990; cited in Dance and Zac-Dance, 1996) starts by categorizing elements of the spoken performance of a presenter. He describes these as the presenter's overt performance. These categories or descriptors include many of the attributes of oratory developed by Aristotle and identified as important by presenters today (absence of fallacies, use of audio-visual aids, taking different spatial and temporal points of view, inventiveness, illusion of spontaneity and many others). Dance then considers the mental competencies that enable the presenter's overt performance to exist. He describes the competencies of memory, flexibility, analysis, imagination, and others, as covert mental processes, all studied extensively in the field of psychology. Dance then attempts to relate his spoken language performance descriptors to the range of *higher mental process competencies*, and in so doing, creates a comprehensive theoretical framework within which presentation skills may be analysed.

Actually the word *analyse* is not the best word here. A distinctive feature of Dance's theory, one that is easily ignored but potentially very important to those intent on improving their presentation skills, is that it supports the idea that analysis can lead to *improvement*. One example will suffice. Dance points out that critical feedback to a presenter is based on an audience's perception of the presenter's spoken performance. Most often this feedback is used by the presenter to improve a particular aspect of spoken performance. For example, a common feedback element is to advise the presenter to provide more examples. Examples often allow the audience to picture what the presenter is trying to say, but only when the examples relate to the experience and interests of the audience. So the feedback is really asking the presenter to think more about the position, experience and needs of the audience. (Dance and others use the term 'decentering' for this process (decentre in UK English); the concept originated in the work of Piaget on child development.) Dance argues that decentring requires the presenter to acquire or develop a higher mental process competence. So critical feedback, based on a presenter's spoken language, and provided as spoken language, is likely to be effective via the development of a mental competence in the presenter. My own interpretation of Dance's approach is that it is relatively easy to respond to the demand for more examples, but much tougher for a presenter to think in advance about the needs of an audience and to put herself or himself in the position of the audience whilst preparing the presentation. To do this the presenter must think of the audience as the 'centre' of the presentation. This in turn requires the development of a specific mental competence. Dance provides many examples of factors that tend to promote, or suppress, decentring. Dance admits that it is difficult to align specific conceptual competencies with specific spoken language performance behaviours (Dance and Zac-Dance, 1996: 333) and future research will be necessary to produce reliable matches; but I do like these ideas and I think that the theory has much to offer us.

Dance's theories focus on the presenter but it is important for us to consider the theoretical foundations of the impact of a presentation on individuals in the audience. Although several approaches are possible here, the one that I would like to explore is based in the area of learning. Learning is not necessarily the only important outcome from a successful presentation, but is important. We may not be using our presentation to teach in a conventional sense, but we do want individuals in the audience to think about what we say and perhaps remember aspects of our argument. Learning theories are central to developments in education but one recent theory stands out for its apparent simplicity and broad application. Kolb (1984) suggested that experiential learning takes place in four phases: experiencing some activity or event; reflecting on that experience; conceptualizing the experience to develop new perspectives; experimenting with these new perspectives. The phases are often described as a 'learning cycle'. It is possible to use this theory to design a presentation so as to provide an initial experience, followed by opportunities for reflection, conceptualization and experimentation. It is also possible to design presentations that provide one experience, followed by another and then another and another. I think that Kolb got it right. I also think that many presenters intuitively design their presentation to provide a learning cycle.

How else can the literature help us?: eye contact

Good ideas aside, the literature also has a role in disseminating the evidence that supports or refutes the theories and the commonly held perceptions of good or poor practice in making presentations. We considered some theory in the section above and we attempted to reach an understanding of what contributes to the common sense and personal experience approach to good or poor practice in Chapter 1. One example here will help us to look at the evidence base in a little more detail.

Here is a commonly held view:

It is really important for the presenter to maintain 'eye contact' with the audience.

Is it? Who says that it is? In fact just about every book on presentation suggests that it is. Here are two examples. Claudyne Wilder and Jennifer Rotondo say: 'Your audience will feel that you are really communicating when you look at each person. Your eyes give away your thoughts and feelings' (Wilder and Rotondo, 2002: 172). And George Brown says: 'Eye movement and contact not only convey enthusiasm and interest, they also enable you to monitor whether you are being understood' (Brown, 1978: 24). In another area, the advice given to trainee teachers almost universally supports the power of eye contact. Can eye contact really do all this? How do they know? Is this fact, hypothesis, personal experience or extrapolation from slim evidence? What literature is available on these concerns; what is it based on and what does it say?

Actually, the literature on the importance and role of eye contact in communication is impressive. Michael Argyle provided a significant analysis of the evidence that supports the importance of eye contact to interpersonal behaviour as early as 1967 (reviewed in Argyle, 1974). Psychologists have noted significant correlation between direction of gaze and pattern of speech and stress the importance of gaze signals in synchronizing communication. There is evidence to suggest that speakers look while talking to gather information, or feedback, from their audience. There is also substantial evidence that people look to send signals as a form of non-verbal communication (or body language), that most listeners find some eye contact rewarding and that too much eye contact can create audience-anxiety. Exactly where evidence ends and conjecture begins is difficult to say but the study and exploitation of body language is a significant endeavour in some settings.

On balance I think that there probably is some evidence to support the statements made by Wilder, Rotondo and Brown but exactly how applicable this evidence is to the circumstances of your presentation is less clear. It might be that some extrapolation is involved. There is, for example, some evidence to support the application of these ideas to presentation and education, but it is not totally convincing. George Breed did some interesting experiments in 1971 where he looked at the relationship between lecturer's gaze, audience retention and audience perception of the lecturer. In some experiments there was 'an effect' but in others there was not (Breed, 1971). Another researcher looked at the correlation between student performance, as measured by grade-point average, and students' perceptions of the most important factors promoting effective teaching. The combination of teacher liveliness and eye contact with students ranked third among 41 factors (Papandreou, 1995). The evidence in educational or presentation situations is, therefore, notable but far from decisive. An additional problem is the possibility that there are racial differences in the way that listeners interpret and react to eye contact with teachers and presenters.

What should we make of this? A commonly held perception (that eye contact between presenter and audience helps communication between presenter and audience) has broad academic support in general studies on communication but limited evidence in an educational or presentation setting. If it were that important surely there would be good academic evidence? If eye contact had that much effect surely it would be easy to measure? Apparently not. Let's add something else to the analysis. My own personal experience has demonstrated, to me, the importance of eye contact in presentation settings. Even without irrefutable evidence, I have convinced myself that eye contact is important. Indeed I am convinced that in many cases it is the single most important adjunct to a good presentation. I guess that this makes me a poor social scientist. So be it. I also think that vitamin tablets stop me getting colds and there is very little hard evidence to support that either. Will I be seeing little green men and flying saucers next? Perhaps.

The point here is that the educational and psychology research literature does not hold all of the answers, yet. Some things are difficult to measure or to demonstrate clearly. In the meantime we have to use all the information available to us to come to our own conclusions and do what we can to seek evidence about what works and what does not. But this does not mean that we should suspend our judgement or believe everything that we read about presentation skills.

Why have conferences, seminars and meetings?

I think that it is important for us to ask questions about the role of the forum in which our presentation will be given. Whether this is the annual meeting of a learned society or a regular academic seminar series, it generally entails an audience listening to, and hopefully communicating with, someone worth listening to. We spend a lot of time and money organizing and attending conferences, seminars and meetings. Why? What do we as individuals get from this? Perhaps we should ask what groups of individuals gain, for these are by their nature always group activities. If we understand more about the role of the forum then we may be able to understand better our own role, and design our presentation to fit this role and learn our presentation skills to enable us to deliver to this role.

Again there are substantial areas of social science that have a bearing here, each with a significant literature. I would like to explore briefly two theoretical approaches that I hope can help us. The first provides an insight into how and why communities of academics develop. The second looks at the social construction of knowledge.

Wenger's communities of practice

Wenger, and others, have explored the relationships between individuals and the communities in which they participate. Wenger (2000) describes the concept of a social learning system where the experience of individuals interacts with the competencies of the community to produce social learning. In an academic setting, increases in the social learning of a community represent advances in knowledge or understanding accessible to all who participate in the community.

Wenger proposes that individuals can belong to social learning systems in several ways; they can *engage* with individuals and groups in the community; they can *reflect* on their own position in the social learning system to orient themselves with respect to the community (Wenger uses the term 'imagination' for this act of belonging); and they can *align* themselves with other processes, so that concepts and perspectives become coordinated (Wenger, 2000).

For academic communities it is arguable that conferences and other meetings provide opportunities for all members of the community to belong in all three ways. Conferences and meetings enable participants to engage, reflect and align. Wenger asserts that the success of organizations depends on their ability to structure themselves as social learning systems. It makes sense therefore for conference organizers to encourage participants to engage with each other, to reflect on their own activities and understanding and to provide opportunities for participants to align their own understanding with that of the community. The same surely applies to individual presenters. We should design our presentations to further the cause of social learning in our community of practice.

Wenger gives some sound generic advice about how communities can further their own social learning but points out that communities 'can also learn not to learn. They are the cradles of the human spirit but can also be its cages' (Wenger, 2000: 230). Perhaps each of us can design our presentation to help members of our own academic communities to break out of cages. It does sound a bit melodramatic, I admit; but perhaps worth aiming for!

Social construction of knowledge

This approach delves further into the issue of who or what will benefit from your presentation. A simple interpretation is that your presentation will benefit the audience. You will use your skills to transmit information (perhaps more) to the audience and in the process you will have helped them to know more and possibly to understand better; you to them. Most of us experience another benefit. It is rare for me to prepare a presentation without benefiting myself from the preparation. In designing a presentation for a particular audience, I invariably try to put myself in their position and, in so doing, think about my material from a different perspective. This process helps me. I benefit. If the presentation goes to plan then I will find myself discussing my material with others, either during the presentation, or in the question period, or in a variety of social interactions. Almost always this process benefits the presenter. This is clearly a two-way process and it is well worth designing a presentation to stimulate this discussion. There are other aspects to this process. In my past I have found myself very interested in fairly obscure academic study, where in all probability I am presenting to the only other people on the planet with similar interests (sad but true). The benefit is then not just to me, and to the audience, but to the field of study. Even in larger fields of study there is the notion that your presentation forms part of the process of constructing knowledge so that the process is itself a social construction.

Cognitive psychologists have researched extensively about how individuals acquire knowledge and learn. Currently much emphasis is placed on constructivism as a theoretical basis for how individuals use their experiences to construct their own understanding. One psychologist in particular stands out in attempting to discover how learning in individuals is produced in social situations.

Vygotsky worked in the 1930s to explore social constructivism and his theories did much to stimulate research into how individuals in groups interact with one another to aid individual understanding and the social construction of knowledge. So there is a theoretical basis to how you can, perhaps should, interact with others at conferences; but the concept is probably enough for us here. Social constructivism suggests that your presentation needs to open the way for your audience to interact with you and with your material so that it becomes a social collaborative activity. Within the community there may well be individuals with better and worse (more advanced and less advanced) understanding of the material and your presentation should engage with both ends of this spectrum. You must do your best to ensure that the community learns about your material in a context meaningful to them so that they can relate the experience of your presentation to their wider experiences. Social constructivism, as a theoretical underpinning to the processes underway in your conference, places a great deal of responsibility on you to design and give your presentation effectively!

In recent years Vygotsky's ideas and social constructivism have been important in developing communication in a specific conference setting; online. Online communication between individuals has been possible for many years and is now common place in distance learning settings and in some 'blended learning' situations, where computer-mediated communication is used to support conventional face-to-face teaching. It is also widely used in less formal chatrooms. This area is not, strictly speaking, a topic for this book but it is relevant to us here and it is also an extensively researched area at present. The issue for educational researchers in this area is how to make online discussions more effective contributors to individual and group learning. Ganawardena, Lowe and Anderson (1997), for example, suggested that active construction of knowledge, online, moves through five phases: sharing of information; exploration of inconsistency; negotiation of meaning; synthesis; and then application of new meaning. Similar processes and phases are central to conventional socio-cultural theories of learning. Evidence from the online education world suggests that this social construction of knowledge is possible in well-organized online discussions. Surely it should be easier in well-organized face-to-face discussions at a conference, particularly with your well-designed and well-presented presentation to provide focus and structure? For most conferences that I have been to this would be an optimistic aim; but certainly an admirable aim. Social construction of knowledge may be what we hope conferences and related meetings lead to but we rarely, if ever, evaluate their ability to achieve this.

Why do conferences, seminars and meetings involve presentation?

'OK', you say. So conferences and related meetings are important for many reasons and my presentation has to be designed to do things that were not, initially, obvious, but are probably quite important. I get that, but why do I have to stand up and speak? Why can't I send an e-mail as that seems to work fine online. What is so important about actually speaking?

A good question! In fact the same question is posed in many areas of life. Why is a real teacher better, sometimes, than a good book? Why is online tuition, sometimes, a second best to face-to-face tuition? Why do politicians speak in parliaments throughout the world? The question is probably so big that it is not really fair to pose it in relation to just conferences and meetings. Perhaps it is too big to need an answer. But many have attempted to discover what is so special about the spoken word and research on it represents a substantial area of human endeavour in several fields of study. I turn here again to the work of Dance, not because I think that his theories have particular experimental justification, but because I think that they have great application. Dance, and many others, propose that speech and spoken language interact fundamentally with the construction of conceptual thought in the human mind. Communication can occur in many forms but the spoken word has particular importance. Dance proposes that it is through speech and spoken language that the mind is constructed, cultivated and shared (Dance and Zac-Dance, 1996). Speech has a special place at conferences because it is primarily through spoken words that social interactions lead to social learning and understanding.

Can good presentation skills be taught?

Note that here we turn from the need to learn presentation skills to a question about teaching. Perhaps these skills can be taught. I do have some concerns, however. These relate strongly to my perception of the lack of credible underpinning theory and supporting evidence in presentation skills. Presentation is big business in the world of business. The success of a businessperson may well depend on her or his ability to persuade or to sell. Fair enough. These are practical considerations that do not necessarily benefit from theory. That's business. But presentation is also big business in the world of education. Students in higher education are 'taught' how to make oral presentations in study skills modules. They are also assessed. To make the assessments fair, students are provided with precise details of the assessment criteria used by assessors. These criteria include structure, content, clarity, interest, evidence and preparedness. They also include more personal aspects of presentation including voice intonation, eye contact with the audience and other aspects of body language and use of audio-visual aids. Naturally this book encourages presenters to think about these aspects and this encouragement is supported by the views of many. Practical experience also supports their use. But I will not come and overtly assess your presentation nor would you appreciate it if others did. Let us be in no doubt that there are gaps in the evidence base and that the formulaic application of instruction will probably not work in all situations. I suspect that cookery also has a developing but sketchy theoretical and evidence base but the proof of the pudding is always in the eating and beauty in the eye of the beholder. I hope that there will always be room in presentation for a personal approach that is entirely set against the rules.

Summary

I am still working on the basis that many presentation skills can be learned and that presentations have a significant and positive role in the development of learning communities. I accept that the theoretical foundations for this process are sketchy but a wide range of research in a number of disciplines is adding sound data. I think that we can learn presentation skills and successfully put this learning into practice.

References

Argyle, M. (1974) *The Psychology of Interpersonal Behaviour,* 2nd edn. Harmondsworth, UK: Penguin.
Brown, G. (1978) *Lecturing and Explaining.* London: Methuen.

Breed, G. (1971) *Nonverbal Behavior and Teaching Effectiveness*. Final Report. Washington, DC: Office of Education (DHEW).

Dance, F.E.X. and Zac-Dance, C.C. (1996) *Speaking your Mind: Private Thinking and Public Speaking*, 2nd edn. Dubuque, IA: Kendall/Hunt.

Ganawardena, C.N., Lowe, C.A. and Anderson, T. (1997) 'Analysis of global online debate and the development of an interaction analysis model for examining social construction of knowledge in computer conferencing'; *Journal of Educational Computing Research*, 17 (3): 397–431.

Kolb, D. (1984) *Experiential Learning*. Englewood Cliffs, NJ: Prentice Hall.

Papandreou, A.P. (1995) *Teaching Viewed Through Student Performance and Selected Effectiveness Factors*. Government Research Report: Cyprus (ERIC accession no. 392760).

Wenger, E. (2000) 'Communities of practice and social learning systems', *Organization*, 7 (2): 225–46.

Wilder, C. and Rotondo, J. (2002) *Point Click and Wow: A Quick Guide to Brilliant Laptop Presentation*. San Francisco, CA: Wiley.

Reassurance for new presenters

Those new to presenting may not need this chapter to begin with. New presenters are generally, and reasonably, most interested in practical advice on how to present well. After a few presentations, however, most presenters want to improve if possible. Finding that presentation has a theoretical basis and a literature may come as a surprise, but it is reassuring that much helpful advice and many common-sense approaches do have support from the education and psychology literature. It is also helpful to realize that conferences, seminars and related meetings do have a role to play; not just in our own personal development, but in the development of our disciplines. It is worth making an effort to present well.

3

An Introduction To Presentation Aids

Key concepts in this chapter:

▌ Why use presentation aids?

▌ Why use technology to deliver presentation aids?

▌ Scripts and prompt cards.

▌ Whiteboards and flip charts.

▌ The overhead projector.

▌ Photographic slides.

▌ PowerPoint.

▌ Webpages

▌ Mindmaps.

▌ Promoting interaction between presenter and audience.

Let us set the scene for this chapter with a case study. This case is based on a group of academic researchers presenting to a mixed audience. It occurred several years ago. The principles involved, however, are almost universal and could equally apply to a 'roundtable gathering' of undergraduates presenting their share of a team project or to a postgraduate research group meeting.

CASE STUDY 3.1
Presentation aids and the research group presentation

I like this form of presentation. Several key speakers each take turns to say something and then a chairperson, or the lead speaker, leads a discussion. The approach is used in Panel Presentations in a variety of formats. In the case described here, five researchers were describing aspects of their personal contributions to their research group. Each presentation took about 5 minutes. The audience was a mixed group of postgraduate students and staff (including me) from other research and teaching groups.

Speaker A gave a brief and to-the-point description of her research. She spoke well and illustrated her talk by reference to prepared OHP slides. These were clear, printed and readable. Speaker A did not look at me during the presentation but seemed to me to be talking to the row of postgraduate students. After the presentation I thought that I knew something about the research area but very little about what the researcher herself actually did. The presentation did not engage me.

Speaker B started with an apology that she did not have slides to illustrate her presentation. At that point another speaker interjected with the old adage that there are 'two types of presentation; those with slides and those with content'. Speaker B's presentation did indeed have content. She spoke fluently about her topic. I felt involved and drawn in. I got the impression that she plunged us all into the very heart of the major controversy in her research field. I could tell you now what the controversy was and what Speaker B's major contribution was.

Speakers C and D both used slides. C used a PowerPoint presentation, established quickly and almost seamlessly in the handover. D used OHP slides. All slides were clear, typed and relevant. Both speakers managed to interest and involve the audience. I found Speaker C's contribution particularly interesting but this probably reflects my interests and the fact that I thought I understood the topic well. I did struggle with the underlying concepts that Speaker D assumed the audience would have already grasped. Both speakers spoke with passion about their research and established in everyone's mind that they, personally, were making valuable contributions.

Speaker E spoke with no slides. I knew his topic well and I had already attended research presentations by him. I did not need slides to help me but looking around the room I did think that others would have benefited from some sort of visual grounding in the topics described.

What is the take-home message? If you can engage with the audience and communicate what you need to without presentation aids, then you do not need presentation aids. Clearly this will depend on your skills, the nature of the topic, the situation and the skills (and diversity) of the audience. Speaker B did this fine. Speaker A did not manage to do this even with the slides. Deciding whether or not to use presentation aids is an integral element of the design of your presentation.

There are lots of issues to address here. We need to clarify the terminology. We need to address why some presenters want to use presentation aids and some do not. We then need to demystify the use of PowerPoint and related software.

Terminology

Many of the terms used in connection with presentation aids do not appear in standard dictionaries. Even worse, the terms come and go and individuals tend to stick with the terms that they grew up with.

Slides are (photography-based) colour-transparencies, often in 35mm format, that are inserted into a projector and projected onto white screens. They used to have glass protective coverings; nowadays they are just plastic films usually in cardboard mounts. They would be prepared sometimes months in advance of important presentations and guarded carefully. Sometimes the glass broke. Some academics maintained huge collections of slides that they would carry with them to conferences. So entrenched into the mindset of academia have slides become that the term is now used to apply to a range of other presentation aids. The overhead projector (OHP) appeared in most classrooms and at most conferences in the 1980s. Although it is possible to write on film rolls on the OHP, most presenters use OHP transparencies designed to lay flat on the optical stage. Older generations of presenters do refer to prepared OHP transparencies as slides.

Then came PowerPoint, or rather, then came a range of computer-based slide generating software (or slide-ware) of which PowerPoint is the most obvious survivor. Anything (almost) that can find its way onto a computer screen can be shown using PowerPoint.

The generic terms 'audio-visual aids' and 'presentation aids' refer to all of these and to much else besides. Technically a visual aid lacks sound and an audio-visual aid includes sound; but this distinction is rarely maintained. Blackboards, whiteboards, flip charts, pieces of paper, prompt-cards, movies and tape-recorders all fit these generic categories. Here, I will use the term 'presentation aid', unless I am referring to something in particular.

Why use presentation aids?

It has been said that the radio has better pictures than does television. Certainly I can get totally absorbed whilst listening to plays on the radio. I 'paint' wonderful pictures in my mind. The same applies when I listen to a good speaker. A good book can do the same thing and isn't it a shame when a book is adapted for television and somebody else's picture is imposed on your own. I guess that this is an important point. If it doesn't much matter if the picture that is painted is yours or someone else's, then presentations without pictures are fine. If the detail of the pictures, or of the text, is important then presenters probably need more than the power of their oratory to communicate effectively with the audience.

I can draw much from my own experience here. Generally I can be well into a lecture or presentation before I need to use presentation aids. But then I reach a point where I need to communicate something in a way that will empower the audience to follow. Maybe I want to emphasize that my talk is going to open up and split into three sections, each with specific characteristics. I could explain this verbally but experience has convinced me that three subtitles, written on a whiteboard or bullet-pointed on a slide, is a more effective way of doing it. I can then be sure that, when I take a turn in direction, most of the audience will be with me and also they will anticipate that at some point in the future I will be turning back to address the other sections. Maybe I want to build up a complex model during my presentation. I am generally happy to talk about each element without presentation aids but I do need a chalk or marker pen to bring all of the elements together

But this is the tip of a large iceberg. There are many reasons why presenters want to use presentation aids. Some relate to the needs of the presenter even more than to the needs of the audience. For example, what purpose does the neatly-typed script serve when it is unopened and unread by the word-perfect presenter? Of course it is there if it is needed, but its main purpose may be to impress the audience. The script confirms that the presentation is not off-the-cuff but is the carefully-crafted product of diligent preparation. Another interpretation of this, and indeed of the use of presentation aids more generally, is that the aid is being used as a 'crutch' to help the presenter. It might help him to feel confident, it might help his timing, and it might help him to remember what it is he is there to talk about. Some authors do not approve of this and suggest that good presenters should not need crutches, but I disagree profoundly. I like to use tools to help me to do things that I cannot do without them. I cannot take nuts from bolts with my fingers; I need to use a spanner. Nor can I explain complex processes without the use of flow diagrams. Someone else's crutch is my presentation aid. Good choice and good use of presentation aids is all part of good design.

This is also an active area of research in instructional design, education and educational psychology. The multi-media revolution of the 1980s worked on the assumption that learning, comprehension and retention are boosted when multi-sensory channels of communication are used. Research to explore this early contention came in the form of Paivio's Dual Coding Theory in 1986. Paivio suggested that incoming linguistic information is represented in the brain in a verbal coding system, whereas incoming non-verbal pictures, sensations and sounds are represented in a functionally separate coding system. Paivio also suggested that verbal memory traces may be weaker than the other traces and predicted that students should be able to recall image-rich material more readily than verbal material and that information that becomes dually encoded will be most easily memorized. Since then a wealth of research data has supported these ideas. Lapadat and Martin (1994), for example, found that undergraduates were able to recall information better when lectures were illustrated with images than when they were not. Kulhavy (1993) demonstrated that geographical maps helped the recall of associated text. The research field is large and expanding rapidly. Currently research is attempting to identify the key parameters in a unifying theory for selecting instructional visuals and using the data to improve the design of multi-media computer-based learning applications. I am personally happy to continue to use presentation aids in my own presentations and to explore the diversity of what is possible and what works. My own research looks at the contribution of video to learning and the role of technology to deliver, and adapt, video in learning situations (see for example, Shephard, 2003).

Why use technology to deliver presentation aids?

I guess that early man thought that the wheel was technology. In this book I tend to use the term to indicate the use of a computer, or something like it. Of course most people, at this stage, think about PowerPoint and many associate this powerful tool with boredom and bullet points.

Edward Tufte provides some powerful views on the misuse of technology for presentations (with particular concern reserved for PowerPoint and its users):

> **Presentations largely stand or fall on the quality, relevance, and integrity of the content. If your numbers are boring, then you've got the wrong numbers. If your words or images are not on point, making them dance in color won't make them relevant. Audience boredom is usually a content failure, not a decoration failure. (Tufte E, 2003)**

The message here is clear. Don't use technology to decorate dull or inappropriate content.

So what should you use technology for?

I think that computers can aid the presentation of material that would be difficult to present in other ways. I like to use video in my presentations and the only way that I can effectively do that today is to use the computer.

I like to present in a format that is close to the one that I research with and that I use to communicate outside of my presentations. I use e-mail, web pages and Word documents for most of my research activity and much of my teaching, most days. (I also use whiteboards and flip charts for much of my teaching.) I want to make the most of the skills that I am confident in for important presentations. I use computers a lot in my presentations. I also like to experiment in my presentations. For many years I based my presentations around 35mm slides, the whiteboard and interactive devices. Computers offer largely unexplored variation on these and I enjoy the exploration.

For every website and book written to dissuade you from using PowerPoint there are many written to encourage you to try it. The best of these acknowledge the problems associated with poor use of technology and attempt to provide a framework that will work for presenter and audiences. More on this is provided in the section below and in Chapter 4.

How many slides or transparencies?

We need to address this question early on. If you decide to use a machine to show pre-prepared text or images, you need to plan how many separate items to show. This depends on why you chose to use slides or transparencies. Some presenters use just one. This may list just a few phrases or words and each is enough to stimulate the speaker to talk effectively around the topic. This one slide is there to remind the speaker what he or she is there to present, but it is also there to help the audience understand the structure of the presentation. Other audiences need more support than this, or perhaps other presenters need more clues. They may have one slide to illustrate each key stage in an argument or each element of a presentation. I know many presenters who have 'one slide per minute' as a rule of thumb. If the argument develops rapidly and the slides help, then this may be necessary, but often the best advice is to use as few slides as absolutely necessary.

A catalogue of presentation aids

Not everyone will agree with my list of presentation aids set out in this section. Some will consider that a typed script is not really a presentation aid. Perhaps most will not agree that mechanisms to stimulate interaction between the audience and the presenter are aids. Well, please let me argue my case, one or two aids at a time.

Scripts and prompt cards

Most successful presenters, in my experience, do not read from a script. Most academics that I have worked with tend to agree, but it is important to reiterate the subject differences noted in Chapter 1. For many, the only other way to get the presentation word perfect is to write a script and then to memorize it. However, very few individuals are capable of memorizing a substantial presentation and yet still sound convincing when delivering it. I know that actors do it and I would have to admit that there probably are some similarities between the professions. But then most successful presenters somehow manage to present their work to appear as if it were spontaneous. I suspect that even successful actors find this difficult to achieve. Then again some presenters write a script and memorize part of it and have enough natural or learned ability to present the memorized and improvised parts as if they were both spontaneous and seamless. Most of these skills have eluded me. I find it relatively easy to speak spontaneously, in a more or less coherent fashion, but I cannot easily memorize text and if I did, I would find it difficult to present it as if it were not from memory. Still, we all make our choices.

The compromise for many is to use notes, where key elements of text and prompts are displayed, that will help us when we need them. Most often they are our most fundamental and important back-up. There are some 'golden rules' for this approach:

- Use card rather than paper so that it does not make a noise in nervous hands.
- Number the cards clearly in case they get out of order.
- Use large text on the card so that you can read it easily, at a glance.
- PowerPoint has a useful Note Page facility that will be described in more detail below.

Whiteboards and flip charts (and blackboards too)

These are the most basic presentation aids but also the most ubiquitous. It is very unusual to be asked to present in a venue where there is nothing to write on! That does not mean that the process is without problems, however. Most readers will recall some presentation or other where the presenter made a total mess of this simple operation.

In every conference that I attend, I can almost guarantee that some poor speaker will arrive to give a presentation only to find that all of the pens have been removed. Another will find that an indelible pen has been used on the only whiteboard available. Someone else will resort to using his or her sleeve to wipe the whiteboard. Meanwhile, in another room, another speaker will be turning the completely used flip chart over to write on the cardboard backing. As often as not, even when all of the facilities are working, someone somewhere will be writing unreadable text in the dark. Nearly everyone will be using a text size too small for anyone behind the front row. Many will remember to turn the light on and to use a large text size but be so unused to writing on the whiteboard that their text is almost illegible. Just occasionally someone will get it right. Then a few well-chosen words, clearly written on a board or flip chart, can be an excellent aid. Text can be used for emphasis. Words or a diagram can be used to provide a supplementary explanation of a difficult concept. They can be used to record a fact, a date or a number that the speaker will return to later in the presentation. The spoken word may have faded, but the written word remains; guiding the speaker and the audience back to the punch line. I use the whiteboard in this way often. Best of all, boards can be used to develop, signpost and punctuate an argument; a teaching approach descended directly from sticks in the sand.

Presenters can also use written text to encourage the audience to interact. For example, a presenter asks the audience something whilst hovering near to the whiteboard, pen in hand, inviting the audience to offer an input. Even the most uncooperative audience find this approach difficult to resist. Actually this operation is a mainstay of the workshop; perhaps the most interactive of all presentation styles.

Presenters who use these tools well are generally those that spend time teaching. Most lecturers use the whiteboard to supplement their OHP slides. After many years they become adept at writing clear, large text; at using colours for emphasis and for symbolic recognition; at not standing in front of the board whilst writing; at leaving the text on the board for long enough for it to do its job; at spelling correctly whilst under pressure; and at starting and finishing with a clean board.

Chapter 4 will emphasize the need for design here. How you use the whiteboard and what you write on it do have to be designed to be really effective. You may want to look spontaneous but it is generally too risky (depending on your own particular range of talents) to leave this to how you feel on the day. I mentioned one particular problem of mine in the last paragraph, which is, I tend to forget how to spell some simple words when I am nervous. I have no problems with complex technical words; it's the simple ones that get me. But, I overcome this because I plan what I am going to write wherever possible. I plan even simple diagrams – I know where the arrows will go and I will have thought about which colours to use. I will also have in mind that chap in the back row, the one trying to write notes. I need to be sure that he can see what I am writing. Table 3.1 describes these important points and offers advice to those new to using the whiteboard and flip chart in presentations.

Overhead projector (OHP)

I developed a dislike for the overhead projector many years ago. To be more correct I dislike the way that it is often used. Many lecturers and presenters discovered that it is possible to present far more material using OHP transparencies than it ever was using a board, black or white. So they did and many still do. Some expect students, or their audience, to copy it out. Others say to students that they must not copy it but that they should use the paper copies (or nowadays the electronic copies) provided separately. Either way the tool provided the illusion of a productivity leap. Worse still, I even found myself using it in this way. In one term I found myself trying to teach a large group of students in a converted chapel where the only presentation device was the OHP; there was no board. I started to use prepared overhead transparencies but I had doubts about how well I could explain things to students in this way. I have always enjoyed the process of developing an argument or systematically 'dissecting' a topic and this is not easy using prepared slides. Next I tried to write notes on the transparency roll as if I was writing on the blackboard. I got a stiff neck, eyestrain and a strange reaction to the solvents used in the pens. I also had problems with glare. There were large windows that could not be covered. The OHP projected a bright screen; but when placed at a reasonable distance from the screen, in relation to the size of the room, it was not bright enough to compete with sunlight. I hated those lectures, week after week. I doubt that the students enjoyed the process much either. As a result of this, and similar experiences, I continued to base my lectures and presentations on the blackboard, and whiteboard, for longer than many; and transferred some of my affection to the computer far earlier than many.

Perhaps I shouldn't be too hard on myself. Most others, in my experience, are as bad or much worse at using the OHP. One of the truly appalling aspects of OHP use is that some presenters make up slides and then use them for the rest of their academic careers. The slides start off cluttered and unreadable and get

TABLE 3.1
Some advice on the use of whiteboards and flip charts for your presentation.

POTENTIAL PROBLEM	POSSIBLE SOLUTION
No pens	Take at least one black pen with you. This should have a broad 'chisel-tip' point so that it can draw broad lines. If it is a dry-wipe marker it can be used on paper flip charts and on whiteboards. Some mathematicians still need to take chalk with them as blackboards are still widely used in this subject area.
Indelible pen used on whiteboard No board wiper Flip chart empty	Explore the venue before your presentation. If all is not well then find a technician or talk to the session chairperson before your presentation.
Too dark to read	Find out how to illuminate the whiteboard or flip chart before your presentation. Practise using the light switches.
Text too small	Here is a rule of thumb. Letter height needs to be at least 5cm for each 10m distance between board and viewer. You must always think about people in the back row. It is not easy to write legibly this large and many presenters will need to practise.
Text difficult to read	Most audiences find lower-case text easier to read. If your writing is untidy or poorly arranged many people will have problems with it.
Audience cannot read text because the presenter stands in front of it Presenter wipes it off the whiteboard or turns the flip chart over before the audience has finished with it Audience cannot hear the presenter because she or he is speaking into the board	You need to empathize more with your audience (see the discussion on decentering in Chapter 1). Practice writing at arm's length so that you do not obscure it as you write. Plan where you will stand after you have written it and plan when you will need to wipe it off. Flip charts can be torn off and stuck to a suitable surface; but only if you have planned to do this and carry something sticky with you. Plan to separate writing time from talking time.
Inappropriate use of colour	Colour can be used for emphasis but it can also be used to code information. It is confusing if it is used in more than one way.
Spelling errors	As far as possible plan what you will write. If you worry that a particular word that you are about to write will be spelt incorrectly, choose another word!

worse year after year. I have also seen presenters at conferences who, year after year, start their presentation by using introductory slides in this way; yes, they move on to newer slides when they get around to recent results, but by then only the toughest in the audience have remained awake or stayed in the room.

However, it doesn't have to be like that. The OHP is capable of good presentation of carefully crafted slides and some presenters are adept at careful and considerate use of it. Because I dislike the OHP so much I am not the best person to advise others on how to use it, so for this next section I draw heavily on the advice given by others. Waller in her book *Using your overhead projector* (1983) provides a historical perspective on how to do it but this is generally supported by Brown and Race's more recent text on lecturing (Brown and Race, 2002). I guess that the ground rules were established early on and my interpretation of these texts is that the authors are enthusiasts for this tool. Chapter 4 in this book provides general design rules that apply as much to OHP slides as to other presentation aids. Here is my best advice for those contemplating using the OHP for their presentation:

- Consider where you will stand, or sit, relative to the OHP, the screen and the audience. Think about the effects of reflections and glare on the audience, particularly those people who sit near the front but at the sides. These poor folk will see not just your slide but also a reflected image of a window or door. What they can see is often different from what you think you are showing. In a teaching situation it is possible to have some control over where the audience sits, but in a conference situation this is less likely. Sometimes it is necessary for the presenter to work at a disadvantage to maximize the benefits to the audience. Most right-handed presenters will want to stand, or sit, with the OHP to their right whilst facing the audience, and most left-handed presenters will want the OHP on their left. Either way it is sometimes difficult to stay out of the sightline of some members of the audience.
- Consider the problems of the audience in the back rows; will they be able to see the bottom of the screen over the heads of those in the front? In smaller rooms there will always be some sections of the audience who cannot see parts of the screen because of the OHP's projector head. Ideally the screen will be at a height related to the size of the room to minimize this problem, but this is not always the case. Your transparency may be designed to fit the OHP

optical stage, which in turn may be designed to fill the screen, but this is not going to help people who cannot see parts of the screen. You can design smaller transparencies if you have identified the problem in advance. You can adapt on the spot by moving your transparency partly off the OHP stage and so using only the top of the screen. Most presenters do neither and just assume that everyone can see everything.

- Be aware that the image may be distorted; the screen is often not vertical and rarely set at a right-angle to the projector. Distorted text is off-putting; distorted graphs and diagrams are misleading. Most presenters apologize for distorted images and move on. Most audiences learned to accept the consequences of this poor design long ago. However, I never got used to this and I spent time adjusting the angle of the screen to the wall, the orientation of the projector to the room, and every aspect of OHP control in an effort to get graphs to look the way that the data says they should look, but I rarely succeeded.
- Use well designed slides. The major features of good design are described in Chapter 4. There is much in common with the good design features of other forms of presentation aids, including: using colours consistently; ensuring that you use an adequate text size; and being sure not to show too much text.
- OHP users vary in their recommendations about how to build arguments and show sequential text using the OHP. Some prefer to show it all on one transparency and to describe the points one by one. Others use several transparencies adding them to the stage one at a time to add content sequentially, (these are sometimes referred to as 'overlays'). Others become adept at covering parts of the transparency until they are ready to describe the particular content. Some suggest that there are sound pedagogic rationales for particular approaches. Some think that too much text all at once will confuse while others worry that attempts to cover parts of the argument will annoy. I suspect that there are subject differences here. In some subject areas the audience will appreciate a step-by-step striptease of the content. I also think that many people developed their sequential explaining-behaviours whilst using boards; then they discovered that the OHP allowed them to present everything at once; and then they realized that this did not match the way that they had learned to explain things. Meanwhile a new generation of explainers came along (who never used a board to help explain) and found

their own new approaches with this new tool. These clever people use overlays or opaque covers with confidence and dexterity to explain things sequentially. So it's also a generation thing! But, yes, I admit, I am biased. I know mathematicians who still use the blackboard to develop their arguments. Many have tried other tools and yet return to the blackboard. Nearly all are highly proficient users of the most complex computing technology imaginable; yet they choose to present their work to students and peers using an ancient technology. I think that this is good, honest professionalism at its best.

So, here we have a near ubiquitous presentation tool, used effectively by a few and badly by many. It often projects poorly focused, distorted images onto a screen that waves about in the wind, is set at an angle, and in an inconvenient part of the room. At least half of the audience can only see the top of the screen, and some of the rest have their view obscured by the projector head. To use it well you need to design your slides in relation to not only your subject and your audience, but also to the situation in which it will be used; something impossible for most presenters in most conferences.

Should the OHP be relegated to the dustbin? Certainly not! In my view the OHP is an excellent back-up device. If you are a well-prepared presenter you will be able to use the OHP as a fall back when more modern technology lets you down. Despite all of my reservations about the OHP, the fact that it is usually there and usually works makes a big difference to me. So, let's learn how to use the OHP well but then keep it in reserve (a little like the starting handle on older cars; we should not have lost those).

35mm slides

Many years ago 35mm slides were very important for presentations, particularly at conferences. Some years ago an eminent scientist left his academic profession to become a Vice Chancellor. His research topic and subject area were related to my interests and he gave me his large slide collection, together with a light box (a large box with a light bulb in it to illuminate the slides laid on its surface). Even with the light box I found the process of sorting the collection too great for me. Also, I think that slides, and other presentation aids, rapidly date and the scientist's research, while important, was in the past. Slides are also quite personal as we all have our own particular approaches to explaining things, so I found that I was unable to use any of the slides.

However, I have my own slide collection. Originally, I used slides to provide colour photographs of apparatus and organisms (I was, after all, a biologist). I also used slides to illustrate environments and literally to 'set the scene' for my presentations, and also to show prepared diagrams that would be difficult to draw on a board. But all of this, like my Vice Chancellor's collection, is now a thing of the past. Nowadays if I want to show a photograph I use a digital system to present it (although it might start off as a 35mm colour transparency). If I want to show a graph I can often construct it in front of the audience electronically. Many people have converted their 'old' slides into PowerPoint slides. None of my old slides are really up-to-date enough to do this. Unless someone asks me for a historical perspective on my research career, my academic slide collection will probably remain in its box.

Slides always have their problems. At every conference that I attended someone will struggle to use a slide with a broken mount. Someone else will find that every slide jams. Yet another poor presenter will discover that the important slide appears upside down. Several presenters will look away from their wonderful image to see that half of the audience is asleep (darkness, combined with Professor Smith's holiday snaps of Roman ruins does this to most delegates, particularly after lunch).

If you do use 35mm slides to illustrate your presentation the conventional tips on how to do it are given below.

- Make sure that your slides will work in the projector that will be available at the presentation. Slides do get jammed easily. Different slides seem to be made for different makes of projector and different designs of carousel. The only solution is to ask about the make of projector that will be available and to test your slides before you go. Sometimes you can take your own tried and tested carousel.

- Most projector carousels take slides that are mounted in 50mm (approximately 2 inch) square mounts. The photograph within is usually 24mm by 36mm mounted horizontally, in landscape format, or vertically in portrait format. If you show slides in portrait format the tall, thin image will project higher and lower than landscape projections. The lower part may be below the screen and not visible to any members of the audience with heads in front of them. The higher part will sometimes appear on the ceiling. So, stick to landscape unless you have some control over how the room and projector is set up.

- Insist on being able to focus your slides yourself. You know what they should look like. In my experience no one else can focus your slides as well as you can. Most remote controls do have a focus knob, so practise with it and check that all parts of the slide are as focused as possible and appear to be in focus from different parts of the room. Where slides in a carousel have different mounts, it will be necessary to refocus at each change.

- Make sure that the slides all project the right way up. If your slides have been professionally mounted and will be loaded by a technician then they will probably be projected correctly. If you do either of these operations yourself then it is important that you mark each slide's mount with an indicator dot to identify the top right-hand corner of the slide. My own rule of thumb is to then turn the slide upside down and back to front before inserting it into the carousel. Experience has taught me that the only way to be sure that the slides will work out right is to test them. Insist on checking each and every slide in the break before your presentation. If you do not do that then at some point in time a slide will be projected incorrectly. This is unnecessary and always embarrassing.

- As with other presentation aids, limit the number of slides to that necessary to illustrate your presentation.

- Be in control of the lights, but do not plunge the room into darkness from the beginning to the end of your presentation.

PowerPoint

My scorn for the OHP is nothing compared to the hatred that some reserve for PowerPoint and related 'slide ware'. Edward Tufte's views are, I guess, encapsulated in the title of his article quoted earlier – 'PowerPoint Is Evil. Power Corrupts. PowerPoint Corrupts Absolutely' (Tufte, 2003). Most presenters enjoy reading Peter Norvig's slightly more subtle Gettysburg PowerPoint Presentation

(Norvig, 2000). There is no doubt that the use of this software as a presentation aid produces a lot of anger and frustration in some people.

Yet these are just tools. No, not *just* tools. Tools are important to us. Some would even say that the ability to make and use tools defines humans as something more than other animals (the argument starts with the evolution of opposable thumbs). Misuse of tools, or the application of the wrong tool, produces incredible aggression in many areas of life. (Can a mechanical hedge trimmer ever yield as good a result as hand operated shears?) Tools are important and how we use them defines our professionalism.

So the issues are important and we must address them. First, I think we should get PowerPoint out of our system before we move onto other computer-based devices.

What you can do with PowerPoint

PowerPoint is one of the most effective and versatile pieces of software that I know. You can use it in its outline mode to import text from, for example, a Word document. You can sort the text into 'chunks' and dispense with content that you do not want, to leave key text that could form titles and bullet points. You can promote and demote items to a range of levels as you explore the content. I have used PowerPoint to plan important documents that will never be produced as presentations as it is a good design tool for some purposes. You can use it in slide sorter mode to scan through your slides and decide which to show today. You can easily insert hyperlinks to online web pages or to images. You can import Excel tables and charts and modify them to suit your presentation style. You can add audio and video clips, or link to either, stored as separate files elsewhere. Playing a short audio interview is a powerful presentation technique in many subject areas made easy with PowerPoint. You can design your own colour scheme and choose from a wide variety of fonts. You can check your spelling (very important for me). You can even modify aspects of your presentation aids at the last minute if you discover that the speaker before you said something important. I have seen the use of PowerPoint raise the confidence of a nervous academic, from being a hesitant presenter to a successful presenter; perhaps not to an inspiring performer, but a successful one. I like PowerPoint a lot.

What some people dislike about PowerPoint

PowerPoint can be used to illustrate some of the most ineffective and dull presentations imaginable. 'Death by PowerPoint' is a term widely used in conferences where presentation after presentation is consistently dull, illustrated by nothing but titles, charts and bullet points on a mid-blue background. Perhaps worse, PowerPoint can be used to do more than illustrate a presentation. PowerPoint often comes to dominate the presentation rather than support it. Attention is transferred from the presenter to the screen. The screen then becomes the focus for the presentation itself. I think that more than anything this is what people really object to.

Objections take many forms. Some suggest that the visual aids generated using PowerPoint obscure rather than enhance the points being made. Some complain that PowerPoint enables presenters to enhance format and presentation to the extent that it overshadows content. Some suggest that PowerPoint imposes a cognitive style induced by linear bullet points, each containing so few words that many are needed to generate arguments. Large numbers of slides, each with a linear array of points, makes it difficult for the audience to evaluate relationships and place content in context. Some dislike the very look and feel of the text and charts generated or displayed by PowerPoint.

Established rules for the use of PowerPoint

There are established 'rules' for using PowerPoint. Perhaps 'rules' is too strong a word and 'guidelines' would be better. Microsoft themselves make a lot of these rules or guidelines available via their website (http://office.microsoft.com). You can be sure that the advice here is endorsed by Microsoft and matches the design of PowerPoint itself. For example, when I looked at the site today (16 January 2004) I browsed through guides on choosing the right colour (sorry, color) for my PowerPoint Presentation and on using the ever-expanding range of design templates.

There are also many texts that attempt to help presenters use PowerPoint and related software. I referred to Wilder and Rotondo's *Point Click and Wow* (2002) in Chapter 2. It is a good book and covers many aspects of the design of presentations with a focus on PowerPoint delivered by the presenter's laptop. Also, I often turn to the education literature for additional ideas and advice and a different perspective on the rules. In the UK, for example, a publicly funded project, the Application of Presentation Technologies Project, looked at the way academics in higher education were using presentation technologies and produced a website that offers advice and ideas (APT, 1999). The site has an academic, rather than a commercial, focus. I particularly like the range of case studies that illustrate how academic staff are using presentation technologies.

So, what are the established rules? (I concentrate here on rules for PowerPoint and related technologies. Generic rules for presentation aids are discussed in depth in Chapter 4.) Of course these rules will vary from time to time and between academic and commercial sources but generally people recommend that:

- Slides should be restricted to 4 or 5 bullet points.
- Each bullet point should be a short phrase or a few words that you can build on.
- Charts and graphs are better than tables of data.
- Graphs should show trends rather than the detail of the data points.
- Do not use elaborate transition effects or sounds.
- Use animations sparingly.
- Use colours, fonts and designs consistently.
- Use large fonts that will be readable by everyone in the audience (some suggest as large as 24 point as a minimum).
- Punctuate and use cases consistently.

Then in relation to how the slides are used:

- Do not allow the slides to dominate your presentation.
- Do not read the text on the slide to the audience.

Now here is a difficult point for me. I understand where these ideas come from and I agree with all of them in many circumstances. However, I disagree with some of them as general rules and I think that most presenters would be wise to make up their own minds about how to use PowerPoint.

Break the rules and decide how you want to use PowerPoint!

Some presenters are very nervous about presenting to large audiences. For many researchers, presentation is part of the job, but not necessarily the most important part of the job. These people do not consider themselves to be 'professional presenters' but professional historians, social scientists or statisticians. If PowerPoint helps them to present in a reasonable manner then I always advise them to break whatever rule is necessary to get their point across. If that means reading the slides then so be it! If you are a sprinter then you do not need crutches. If you are a bit wobbly on your legs then at least a walking stick is a good idea.

Data presentation

Some subject areas have taken PowerPoint to new heights, or depths, of data presentation. There is a definite subject difference in what is considered acceptable. Social scientists, for example, tend to like relatively simple graphs that obey the rules: axes are clearly marked with large fonts; the lines mark trends; short equations appended to the lines indicate goodness of fit and other characteristics. Where possible, data is translated into pie charts and bar histograms for ease of interpretation. Social scientists are used to this level of 'clarity'. In my experience, engineers and material scientists demand far more from a visual representation. They want to see all the data that contributes to a trend. They want multiple curves plotted on the same axes so that each variable can be plotted against temperature, pressure and the time of day! They are happy with very small, almost illegible text to mark axes, on the grounds that anyone able to understand the presentation will know what the legends are. They also want the slide to show elements of the experimental procedure and perhaps a photograph of the state of the product when it failed. These visuals break many of the rules but they work for some professions because that is the style that these professionals are used to.

Actually, the above description of a graphic slide, given here almost as a parody, has some points in common with the recommendations given by Edward Tufte in his ground-breaking book, *The Visual Display of Quantitative Information* (1983). I have great sympathy here because I like this sort of graphic but I also know that many do not. In my experience some professions actually prefer to see the data in tables rather than translated into graphs and charts. Mathematicians and statisticians appear to be quite capable of drawing pictures of data sets in their minds. To be accurate this is not really a PowerPoint issue. PowerPoint is powerful enough to allow almost any graphic to be projected. Many of the problems come from the software used to produce the image in the first place.

Because most people use Microsoft Excel to produce graphs and charts to display in Microsoft PowerPoint, the graphs and charts have a Microsoft look and feel. If this is right for you and your audience then use it; if it is not, then do not use it for convenience at the risk of alienating your audience! Most quantitative subjects have their own data analysis software that will produce graphics that will fit your particular style. Dare I say that there is still room for the hand-crafted graphic? PowerPoint then is just the delivery vehicle. For now we must work on the basis that there are differences of opinion about how data should be presented in PowerPoint.

Bullet points

Some people hate bullet points on principle. The process of distilling a complex argument into a few points, and then capturing each point as a short phrase, is helpful for some but not for others. I think that, to a point, this depends on how you like to explain things. Much of this book has been constructed in bullet point format, but with text added to support the bare bullets. However, this is not the only possible approach. I have experienced many excellent bullet-point-free presentations given with and without PowerPoint. Again, do not let the convenience of bullet-pointing force you into alienating your audience. PowerPoint has many other 'page layouts' that should allow you to design your presentation without the use of bullet points – but there are also other viable alternatives to PowerPoint!

Alternatives to PowerPoint

Yes, there is the possibility of a presentation aid that does not involve PowerPoint! I describe here two developments that I hope presenters will try.

Web pages

Web pages probably need no introduction. They are widely used by academics, businesses and government to communicate and inform via a computer. They are evolving rapidly (at least I hope they are because at the moment they are by no means satisfactory for all purposes). Many presentations nowadays also rely on the computer to generate an image to project as a presentation aid. For some years now it has been possible, even routine, to save your PowerPoint presentation so that it can be delivered via your website. Sometimes the result is that presenters move from a relatively rich audio-visual medium (the web page) to a relatively poor one (the PowerPoint slide). In fact, web pages can do most things that PowerPoint slides can do with the advantage that they do not, generally, look like PowerPoint slides. So, design some of your web pages to act as presentation aids, and the next time you give a presentation insist that you have access to a laptop linked to both the Internet and a video-projector. Most presentations that I give nowadays use web pages to deliver presentation aids, but at the moment it is difficult to predict how this area will develop.

Mind maps and related devices

Some educationalists suggest that mind maps are excellent study aids for visual learners. There is a lot of education theory hidden in this statement, and as you can imagine, quite a bit of controversy. For many, the process of creating mind maps stimulates creative thinking, enhances recall and helps decision-making. There may be links to constructivist approaches to learning. Nancy Margulies (2002) offers a useful, non-commercial, introduction to mind maps and visual mapping. Mind maps are also big business and there are a number of software products that allow authors to create and present with mind maps. One example that I have successfully used is *Mindmanager* (2004). Figure 3.1 provides an example of a mind map written using *Mindmanager* and designed to help explain the structure of this chapter. While much educational research is underway to explore how mind maps help learners, there is less research information, if any, on how good a tool they are for presentation. I hope that some serious research will be attempted in the future. There is no doubt that these tools do facilitate a 'holistic' observation (perhaps analysis) of systems and structures but sometimes they do appear to be just lists of bullet points spread around the same page rather than sequentially on different pages. Perhaps I am missing the point.

As a scientist I have, of course, used a wide range of related tools throughout my career and presented using some of them. I have often used flow diagrams to build visual and mathematical models and working simulations of complex processes. I have also used concept maps to explore interactions between elements. I am all for exploration.

FIGURE 3.1

An expanded mind map of Chapter 3 produced using *Mindmanager* software. Presenters can use the mind map in presentation mode. In this format, small parts of the screen can be enlarged or reduced, topics and subtopics can be condensed and expanded and links can be made to text, images and other resources.

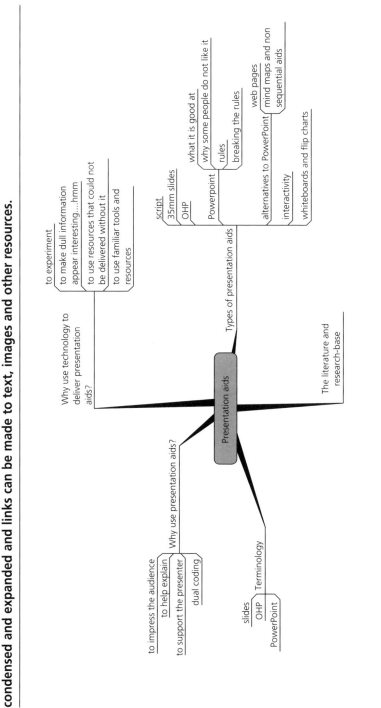

Devices for interactivity

The best presentation aid that I know of is one that allows the presenter to interact with the audience. I think that presentations should always engage the audience to the point that they feel part of it and not peripheral to it.

Some presentation aids provide opportunities for the presenter to seek audience participation. It is easy to show a picture and ask members of the audience to describe it, or comment on it, or interpret aspects of it. In general this is more to do with the use of examples relevant to the audience than it is to the presentation aid itself. There are, of course, many other ways to provide relevant examples.

Another approach that improves interaction with the audience and that relates to the use of presentation aids is to move around. Not everyone can do this happily. Many people, and some subject areas, dictate that the presenter will be fixed to a spot at the front of the room. Unless the setting is very formal I like to move around if I can. I like to move into the audience and look at my presentation aids from their perspective. This way I can check that I can see what I want them to see. More importantly it demonstrates my empathy with the audience and is itself a form of interaction.

As described in previous chapters, most presenters do feel that eye contact with the audience is the most important aspect of interactivity. The aid, of course, is not on a piece of paper nor is it in the computer. It is in you. Whether you are an established academic or an undergraduate student, you will want to give the best presentation possible. Your eyes are the best presentation aid that you have (though your voice is important too!).

Interaction is really important to your presentation. It will be considered again in Chapters 4, 5 and 8.

Summary

However we define presentation aids, there is no doubt that they can be useful to the audience and to you as a presenter. All presentation aids carry with them a burden of preparation and practice, but some more than others. I do hope that presenters who want or need to use technology will look beyond PowerPoint, but in the process not overlook the adaptability and usability of this remarkable presentation software. The next chapter examines how we design our presentation, with or without presentation aids.

References

Application of Presentation Technologies in UK Higher Education (1999) APT project web site http://www2.umist.ac.uk/isd/lwt/apt/home.htm (accessed 15 December 2003).

Brown, S. and Race, P. (2002) *Lecturing*. London: RoutledgeFalmer.

Kulhavy, R.W. (1993) 'How geographic maps increase recall of instructional text', *Educational Technology, Research and Development,* 41 (4): 47–62.

Lapadat, J.C. and Martin, J. (1994) 'The role of episodic memory in learning from university lectures', *Contemporary Educational Psychology*, 19 (3): 251–376.

Margulies, N. (2002) *Mapping Inner Space: Learning and Teaching Visual Mapping,* 2nd edn. Tucson, AZ: Zephyr Press.

Mindmanager (2004) *Mindjet's visual tool for brainstorming and planning,* http://www.mindjet.com/uk/index.php (accessed 21 January 2004).

Norvig, P. (2000) *The Gettysburg Powerpoint Presentation,* http://www.norvig.com/Gettysburg/ (accessed 16 January 2004).

Paivio, A. (1986) *Mental Representation: A Dual Coding Approach*. Oxford: Oxford University Press.

Shephard, K.L. (2003) 'Questioning, promoting and evaluating the use of streaming video to support student learning', *British Journal of Educational Technology,* 34 (3): 297–310.

Tufte, E.R. (1983) *The Visual Display of Quantitative Information.* Cheshire, CT: Graphics Press.

Tufte, E.R. (2003) 'PowerPoint Is Evil. Power Corrupts. PowerPoint Corrupts Absolutely', *Wired,* September 2003 (http://www.wired.com/wired/archive/11.09/ppt2.html; accessed 9 January 2004).

Waller, C. (1983) *Using Your Overhead Projector and Other Visual Aids*. London. Fordigraph Ofrex.

Wilder, C. and Rotondo, J. (2002) *Point Click and Wow: A Quick Guide to Brilliant Laptop Presentation*. San Francisco, CA: Wiley.

Presentation aids for new presenters

Presenters do not have to use presentation aids and those who want to, do not have to use technology to deliver them. But presentation aids can:

- help you to explain;
- help you to support understanding by the audience;
- help you to organize and deliver your presentation;
- help you to interact with your audience.

Technology can help you to deliver a wide range of presentation aids that may help your audience and you.

Whatever presentation aids you adopt, you do have to acquire a range of skills to make them work for you. One of the most straightforward yet versatile is PowerPoint; but there are many others that you should not ignore.

4

Designing and Writing a Presentation

Key concepts in this chapter:

∎ Types of presentations that you might be invited to give.

∎ How to decide what your presentation style should be.

∎ Establishing expectations and outcomes.

∎ Presenting at a level and pace to suit the audience.

∎ Designing the right structure for the audience.

∎ How to interact with the audience.

∎ How you should present yourself to the audience.

∎ Presentation aids that help you and the audience.

This chapter addresses the elements of presentation design established in Chapter 1 as those most likely to separate good presentations from bad presentations in the eyes of the audience. Before we get to content, structure, self-presentation, interaction and presentation aids we should consider the types of presentation that you are interested in and the considerations that will influence your design.

What type of presentation will it be?

We start with a consideration of the different types of presentation that most of us will encounter. If you are an undergraduate then you are probably planning for a project research presentation. If you are a practising professional then you may have to give a short lecture or even a keynote presentation at a major conference. There are design considerations that are common to all presentations, but some relate only to particular presentations.

Poster

The poster presentation is perhaps the most likely first encounter for young academics or other professionals. Most professional bodies run conferences that provide opportunities for conventional conference presentations and for poster presentations. For some the poster presentation is a second best, especially if you didn't get your paper accepted for the full conference. This is a shame because poster presentations do provide a different opportunity for presenters. Some see poster presentations as a diversion from the main conference, providing delegates with an opportunity to relax, after a hard day's listening, whilst wandering around the poster hall drinking wine. Again this is a shame. It is actually quite difficult to give a serious presentation to tipsy conference delegates.

So, what are posters good for? Certainly, you can put in a lot of preparation 'up front' and you have to feel that this is worthwhile. In general the audience in front of you will be much smaller than in a large lecture room; sometimes a single person; sometimes a small group. Sometimes you can comment on your poster repeatedly within the session and in other circumstances you are asked to give a short presentation at fixed times. Either is fine.

Guidance on how to produce your poster is provided in Figure 4.1. Generally the process of talking around the poster is quite straightforward. You have a small group in front of you who have come to your poster because they are interested in it. Be prepared for a conversation rather than a formal delivery. You can relax. Don't prepare a script but certainly think in advance about the key elements. More so than with other presentations, be prepared to be flexible. Have some handouts prepared in advance. Be keen to engage in discussion. Enjoy it, but don't drink too much beforehand!

Panel

Panel presentations are relatively new. Several relatively well known people sit at the front of the room and, in turn, deliver a short presentation. Sometimes the presentations are illustrated using visual aids but sometimes the presenters just chat. There is a lot to be said for careful design of these panels. Ideally not

FIGURE 4.1

Some information about producing a poster.

Designing a poster

First find out from the organizers how much space you will have, what shape it will be and how the poster will attach to it. Typically it will be 1m by 1.5m in portrait or landscape format but it is sometimes much larger. Most posters are attached using velcro adhesive discs.

Then find out how much money you can spend. Professionally produced, laminated posters nearly always look better than ones held together with blue tack. Someone is spending a lot of money sending you to the conference; do not skimp on the poster.

Design the text so that the title can be read from 5m distance and the rest from 3m distance. Use a simple, clear font like Arial. The letters in the title need to be 2.5cm tall to be clear. To be eye catching they need to be 5cm tall. Good proportions are also important but difficult to achieve without experimentation.

Design the poster so that it has a clear title across the top, to grab attention. The content should be in vertical columns with as many visually appealing photographs as possible. This poster has too much text!

Produce something that people can take away. Your card? A brief synopsis of your paper? Reprints of your paper? Anything as long as it has your e-mail address and the URL of supporting web resources.

PowerPoint is an excellent tool for producing posters. There is plenty of advice out there on the web; use it. You have to use Page Set-up to input the final dimensions of your poster page. You also need to use the ruler to align your columns, title and pictures or put these into a table. After that it is a good creative experience! © Kerry Shephard

You will need to get your poster printed using an ink-jet plotter designed for the purpose.

everybody on a panel will agree with each other, otherwise panels can be dull. I must admit that designing a panel is quite a challenge. I have tried it and it's not easy. Personalities get in the way. People tend not to do what they said they would do. Often, the panel members promise to support different viewpoints but on the day, they reach amicable agreements. Still, that's life. If you are asked to contribute to a panel you need to find out who else will sit on the panel. You will need to co-ordinate with them what you say and perhaps discuss particular standpoints for each of you to defend. You will also need to discuss strategies for interacting with your audience. You do not want the panel presentation to be a one-way affair. On the whole, panel presentations are good fun.

Keynote

I have never been asked to give a keynote presentation. I think they are a particular challenge. The keynote is often designed to either start off a conference to set the scene for discussion, or to round off the conference to summarize the activities. Both are, I suspect, difficult. It is important for the keynote presenter to have a good idea of what each of the other presenters is going to say, so there is a lot of homework involved. Because the keynote presenters are well known in their fields, they have a reputation to maintain. There is probably much stress involved in providing a good keynote presentation. It has to address issues that the audience is interested in and it can't be too predictable, and it is certainly not something that can be repeated from conference to conference. So as I said, quite a challenge.

Short lecture

Most conference presentations are short lectures. Much of this book is really about the short lecture as this is still the mainstay of the conference and seminar environment, and is relevant to meetings where short presentations are given.

Symposium

The symposium format is not new. Several speakers speak sequentially about a topic or a single area of interest. Sometimes these presentations are gathered together into a book, to reflect current thinking, or recent progress, on a particular theme. A challenge for the presenter here is to produce something that complements what other presenters in the same symposium will present. Communication is needed; communication with the symposium organiser and sometimes communication with other presenters.

Departmental seminar

Departmental seminars are my favourite form of presentation. Generally they occur because somebody has invited you and people are never rude to guests. Generally speaking the audience will be mixed students and staff. Probably everybody will be interested in the topic and very rarely do people come because they have been told to come. The departmental seminar offers the ideal opportunity for presentation. Presentations generally last a reasonable time, say, 45 minutes to an hour; enough time for a beginning, something in the middle and a summary, with sufficient time to stimulate a decent discussion. These events exist to be enjoyed. An ideal opportunity to practise your craft.

Project research presentation

This form of presentation is broader than its title indicates. This is the sort of presentation that is considered to be developmental for the presenter. The presenter is expected to get as much from it as the audience. The presentation may occur in the third year of an undergraduate programme when the student is presenting the results of a research project, or perhaps periodically during a postgraduate training period. The circumstances are similar. The presenter is on show. They have had time to prepare and they will receive feedback whether they want it or not! Most of the feedback will be constructive, but not all. These are an excellent introduction to the art of presentation.

Research group presentation

This also is rather a broad area. On the face of it you might think that this is less challenging than the typical research presentation for, after all, you are a member of a team or group and they are all on your side. But don't believe it! Research groups, like any other groups, are made up of individuals. They have a broad range of interest in what you have done and probably also quite a range of understanding of what you have done. You might find it difficult to describe the detail and the rationale to everybody, but everybody will offer feedback. In postgraduate research-group presentations there might be a lot at stake. Your research group may have been endeavouring for many years on a particular problem and every small contribution is very important. Others will build on what you have done. Never underestimate the importance of these events to other people in the group as well as to yourself.

Presenting in groups

Undergraduates nowadays are encouraged to develop group skills and there is no doubt that group-working skills will be important when you come to give a group presentation. But do not underestimate the problems that you might experience. There are two sorts of groups: those that you do work well with and those that you do not. Personalities play a huge part in deciding what your group can do and what it should not attempt. Individuals have different views on the importance of meeting deadlines. They have different values with regard to the equitable sharing of workload. Individuals will have different appreciation of their own skills. Agreeing on what your group is to say may be difficult. Agreeing on who says what in the presentation may be difficult. Sometimes conflicts or disagreements within a group can lead to 'creative tensions'. More usually in my experience they lead to destruction. Most undergraduate groups will benefit from careful guidance by a tutor or facilitator. In the wider world we have to find our own way through group dynamics.

If you find yourself in a group that you get on with, enjoy it. This is a great experience and you will all share the benefits of a successful presentation. However, if you find yourself in a group with difficulties, my best advice is to try hard to find one member of the group willing to lead the presentation. Sometimes this leader will be the person who initiated the project and sometimes it will be an elected person. But it is important to recognize that without a lead person, individuals within the group might continue to disagree until they drop out. Somebody with leadership skills may be able to hold the whole thing together for long enough to get you through the presentation!

Intercultural communication

There are aspects of communication or presentation that must be influenced by cultural differences in, for example, non-verbal communication. Some of these differences have been identified by psychologists and described, for example, by Michael Argyle (1988). There are clearly documented differences in the use of gesture, facial expression, eye contact, spatial behaviour, touch and posture between different cultures. I have been fortunate enough to present at conferences and in other settings in the UK, Norway, Holland, Australia, New Zealand, the USA and Canada. Although on many occasions the audiences have been multicultural, I do not remember an occasion when everybody in the audience was from a different culture than my own. I have never had to pretend to be anything that I was not. Where the audience is multicultural, it is difficult to apply any knowledge about cultural differences that you may have, to benefit any particular group. The best advice that I can give is to be you.

Where the audience is mostly from a different culture than your own, then a different strategy may be necessary; but perhaps not. Remember that I am on new territory here. Clearly it would make sense to discover a significant taboo, before the presentation, rather than after it. But it is difficult for a presenter to remember a whole range of new do's and don'ts for each presentation. Many aspects of non-verbal communication, for example, are difficult to control consciously. The effort may be too much, even if you know what to avoid and how to do it. Perhaps someone will invite me to speak in Japan or Iceland. If so, please tell me what I really must avoid doing but also please forgive me if I do it anyway. I will probably be struggling.

Design considerations

Before you design your presentation, consider the basis on which your design rests. As with other design tasks, good design will produce something that excels in many ways. In particular, good design produces something that is functional as well as aesthetically pleasing.

Are you nervous?

I think this is the most important design consideration. Whether you are nervous or not will have a profound effect on how you perform and should therefore have a profound effect on how you design your presentation.

Do your hands shake? If they do, then you really need to find some way to hide this from your audience. If the audience sees your hands shaking excessively, this may well influence their views on you and on your presentation. Of course everybody gets nervous and in stressful circumstances everyone's hands shake slightly; but some people's hands shake tremendously. If this is you, then you need to present without shaking transparencies, rattling prompt cards or quivering pointers. So design your presentation to use a keyboard firmly fixed to a desk, and point using a mouse-operated cursor.

When you present in your nervous state, does your mind go blank, do your lips freeze up, do you stare like a frightened rabbit caught in the headlights? If this is you, then you seriously need a presentation aid; not to help the audience understand what you have to say, but to help you to remember what it is you have to say!

When you present in your nervous state, are you likely to fall over? This is not as silly as it sounds as nervous people in stressful circumstances do tend to fall over. In some lecture theatres it is even possible to fall off a stage. How embarrassing. If this is you, then you may need to design a presentation that can be accomplished from a seated position. Sitting down may not be perfect in some circumstances, but is certainly better than falling over. We have more to say about the subject of nerves in Chapter 5.

Can you use IT resources?

Are you one of those people who really can use IT resources? Can you copy your files onto a floppy disk and be confident that you will be able to upload them again? When you upload them onto a strange computer, and they disappear into the depths of the computer's hard disk, can you find them again? When you show your presentation and all the fonts are different from those that you inserted, can you change them at the last minute? How resourceful are you? If you are fairly resourceful and these things don't seem to worry you, then go for it. IT may well provide the best presentation aid for you. PowerPoint may be perfect for you. If you have problems in these areas, they are likely to become more serious when you are stressed and when you are nervous in front of an audience.

What do the audience expect?

Another important factor that contributes to the design of your presentation relates to audience expectation. Knowing what the audience expects is really part of your task as a presenter, but this is often difficult for new presenters. It is sometimes difficult to predict just how aggressive or how demanding a particular audience is likely to be. Will they ask questions in the middle of your delivery? Even if you ask them not to? You have to research this.

There are many ways to research an audience but I think the best is to ask people, more familiar with the audience than you, what they think the audience expects. Let's say you are going to a conference and some weeks before the conference starts, the programme becomes available. The programme will identify all the other speakers. Phone a few of them and ask them about their experiences of the audience in previous years. How tough will the chairpeople be on timing? What about styles of clothing? Do people stick to casual clothes or will everybody be really smart? Will most presenters be reading a script or will most have remembered their presentation word for word? Does the audience generally frown upon the use of PowerPoint and other visual aids?

I think that it's always challenging to deliver in a way different from that expected by the audience. For example, an audience of mathematicians may well be keen to see your proofs developing on a blackboard. If you present the results more directly as a PowerPoint bullet point they might be disappointed. Audiences used to real data will probably be disappointed if you present them with a fairly simple line graph. Some common sense and your own experience are really important contributions to this aspect of presentation design.

How adventurous are you?

There are two sides to this. There are times when being adventurous and finding new ways to present, and developing new skills on the way, is the right thing to do. But there are some presentation situations where being adventurous, and failing, will damage your career. This is too great a price to pay for personal development! I do like challenges and I do like to try different things, but there are some presentation circumstances in which I'd resort to fairly straightforward, even dull, presentation styles. I save my exploration for circumstances in which failure does not have a huge cost.

Your skills: voice, body language, movements

The last major design factor that we should all consider, relates to our own communication skills or rather how audiences appreciate our skills. How well does your voice carry? Do you squeak or do you bellow? Do you stutter or slur your words? Do you have a wonderful but nevertheless difficult-for-others-to-understand local accent? And what about your body language or non-verbal communication? Will your audience see you as honest, trustworthy and straightforward? Or do you have odd mannerisms that make them wonder about you?

Feedback is really important here. You need to put yourself in situations where people can offer you advice on how you look, how you came across and whether, or not, your non-verbal messages coincided with your verbal messages. If you have problems in this area then you need to design a presentation to overcome the problems or at least hide them. Here is an example. I sometimes get feedback (that I ask for) to tell me that I move my hands too much. This is true. I have even been told that members of the audience find it exhausting just keeping up with me! I know that I can stop moving but I like to move my hands because it helps me explain things better. I like to move my feet because I think that moving around helps me interact with the audience. I think that movement also helps me to expend excess energy. It might be a problem for some but curing the problem would probably be difficult for me. So I design my presentations around this particular aspect of my personality. I make sure that I have things to point at on the screen to occupy my hands for at least some of the time. I make sure that I have space to move and that there is nothing for me to knock over. Design.

Is English your first language?

Our next consideration relates to how good your use of English is. If English is your first language, then it may be as good as it is going to get. It is difficult to change the way that we speak – not impossible, but difficult. You may wish to reflect on how fast you speak and how carefully you pronounce particular words. You might have to think carefully about particular words that you may choose not to use (if for example you mispronounce them when you are stressed); this is part of the design process. But in general there is not an awful lot that you can do.

The real problems in presentation come when English is not your first language or, for English speakers, when you attempt to speak in another language. I have never had to do this, but I have experienced many presentations where the presenter has valiantly been speaking in a language that she or he did not grow up with. This is difficult for the presenter and I think that most audiences really respect the challenges the presenter is overcoming. But it has to be said that the process is also particularly challenging for the audience. It is extremely difficult concentrating on what a presenter is talking about at the same time as trying to understand the presenter; because they have a difficult accent; or because they are slurring their words; or because, let's face it, their use of English is just not good enough for the circumstances in which they find themselves. This is an area where feedback is essential. I would say that there is no point in a presenter going to present at an important conference, unless they are reasonably confident that their use of English is good enough to be understood in the circumstances that they design their presentation to be offered. The best way to get this confidence is to seek feedback from people you trust. As I have described in other chapters in this book, the feedback process is not easy. Sometimes the people that you ask are embarrassed to give you an honest opinion. They are so keen to boost your confidence, as they should, that they suspend their judgement. They do not tell you that they don't understand some words or that your English really isn't good enough yet. This dishonest feedback is no good to you whatsoever. You need constructive, but honest feedback.

There are some things that you can do to help the audience understand you:

- You can speak as clearly as you possibly can. Generally this means slowing down!
- You can use feedback to identify the words and phrases that others cannot understand and where possible design these out of your presentation.
- You can speak facing the audience. If you face the audience then the audience has the maximum chance of understanding what you say.
- You can identify the words that are likely to be problematic and write these on a whiteboard as you say them; even better use PowerPoint and point out the word in question as you speak it.

CASE STUDY 4.1
The postgraduate research group

Bill was an experienced postgraduate supervisor with an excellent record of successful completion. He maintained a research group of three or four postgraduate students and generally managed to get them all to present successfully at the annual conference. Their success depended in no small part on good design and rehearsal at departmental seminars.

In next week's seminar, three postgraduate students were to present aspects of their own projects. The group had discussed this seminar in depth and designed each presentation in relation to the strengths, and weaknesses, of each student. Bill worked on the principle that different presentation styles suited different people but that no one should be content with their existing style. Every presentation provides an opportunity for experimentation, development and confidence building. The trick was to take challenges one at a time. Bill used a presentation checklist to structure the feedback that he would give each student after the seminar. He did not ask each student to give feedback to the others as this had caused problems in the past. Bill was good at giving balanced feedback and was sensitive to most of the problems that young presenters have.

Hilda was the star of the group. She had a first from Oxford and she exuded confidence and ability. Hilda had decided that she would prepare a script but would not need to read from it. She would refer to one or two OHP transparencies but otherwise focus her attention on the audience. Bill had nothing to add.

Lucy was very shy. She had presented before but had always read from a script. Bill was keen to encourage Lucy to limit her reading but he was as concerned as Lucy was that she might dry up completely. Bill's advice was that Lucy should have a script for the start and end of her presentation but that she should focus on some presentation aids for the middle part. His hope was that Lucy's confidence would build in the departmental seminar so that she would read even less at the later conference.

David had great enthusiasm for his topic but he also had problems. Even in conversation he seemed to take long pauses to think and often rambled around his subject. Bill's advice was that David should use carefully constructed prompt cards and that he should practise maintaining a flow without losing his place or wandering off topic. In the event, David chose to use PowerPoint to both produce his prompt cards and show key results to the audience.

The seminar was successful and a learning experience for all three students. Hilda coped well with a minimum of presentation aids but did worry that some of the audience may not have understood the core of her argument. She resolved to show an introductory OHP transparency next time. Lucy coped better than she thought she would and got some encouraging feedback from friends in the audience. She knew that she had to look at people in the audience more but felt more confident about doing this as she gradually reduced her dependency on her written script. David proved to be proficient with PowerPoint. He decided to use it to show more elaborate presentation visuals next time. Bill was content.

Case study 4.1 illustrates the need for individual design; not just in relation to the topic and the venue but particularly in relation to the skills, character and experience of the presenter. If you are a postgraduate student preparing for a big conference, look out for Bill. His experience will be a real asset to you. We should now turn our attention to our five key considerations.

Content

It is really important, as part of the design process, to establish what the audience expects and to identify particular outcomes that you will work towards.

Establishing expectations and outcomes

Many years ago I was asked to give a departmental seminar on my research. I offered what I thought was a descriptive title, made all the necessary preparations and presented as well as I could. After my presentation, my hosts let me know that they were disappointed that I chose to talk about previous research rather than current research. This was a shame. I felt that I let them down. I certainly could have told them about current research but I chose to describe a piece of research that I thought told a better and more complete story. I suspect, but do not know, that this mistake had a long-term effect on my career.

Just as important, is the need for you to think about your own objectives. Most lecturers in higher and further education have no problems nowadays thinking about learning outcomes. Many other presenters, however, might find this a challenge. What do you actually expect your audience to gain from the experience of listening to your presentation and interacting with you? Is the primary objective entertainment? Probably not. Perhaps a significant objective is to help you. If so, then you will need to design in opportunities for feedback. Perhaps you aim for your presentation to be generally informative. If so, it will need to have factual content and be delivered in an interesting manner. You will not be able to give the audience an examination at the end, but you may need to design in some interactions that will enable you to determine how informative your presentation actually was. Perhaps, at the most serious end of things, you expect your presentation to make a serious contribution to socially constructed knowledge. If this is the case, you will need to design it to engage with those in the audience with similar expectations.

Level and pace to suit the audience

'Level and pace to suit the audience' sounds so simple, but it is probably the most difficult aspect of your presentation. Have you attended presentations where you have either had no chance whatsoever of understanding, or have heard it all before? Was that the fault of the presenter or of the audience? What did you think at the time? Research is really important here. Before you design your presentation, you have to research the sort of audience you will encounter. You need to know your subject and you need to know how well your likely audience will know the subject. This is a real challenge even for experienced academics, who sometimes get used to talking to people that know their subject and so find it difficult to speak more generally. Sometimes it is the other way around. I once spoke at a local natural history group meeting on bio-geography. I know that they enjoyed my presentation but they would have enjoyed it more had I realized just how much knowledge and understanding they had of bio-geography. I had underestimated them. It was my first encounter with them so I had some excuse, but I should have done more research. Our 'organized professional' in Case study 1.2 was a master at preparing for 'mixed-ability' audiences. One approach is to ensure that your presentation can be interpreted at more than one level, but this is difficult and does need good design.

Pace is also really important but very difficult to design for. At the design stage you will estimate the amount of material that you can cover in relation to the pace that you think you can maintain and that the audience can keep up with. You may well have to adapt that pace when you start to present! Be aware of your audience. See where they are looking and how they are looking, and adapt your pace accordingly. The main element of design is to be prepared for that adaptation. You may not be able to present as much as you hoped but you still need to summarize at the end. Closure is important. Case study 1.1, about the disorganized professor, is useful here. Simon clearly was prepared to adapt. His disorganization was a 'front' for a well designed presentation.

Choose a suitable title

Title is an important design feature but difficult to advise on. (For example, I have struggled with the title of this book.) In some settings, the title and your name are the only items of information that the potential audience can use to decide whether to attend or not. The title can dictate whether you get the right audience, the wrong audience or no audience! Some presenters refuse to use anything other than a factual title. Others are happy to gloss a dull topic with an attractive title. Some presentations will find it difficult to attract an audience no matter what they are named. Like so much else, it is your choice. Seek advice from colleagues and bounce a few ideas around.

I once travelled from New Zealand to Adelaide to present at a conference to an audience of three. Perhaps I needed a more attractive title than 'Diffusion gradients in unstirred mucous layers'.

Structure

Chapter 1, I hope, convinced you that your audience will appreciate your presentation best if they can understand its structure. Audiences like to know where the presentation is going and when it will end. Many individuals like to be able to take notes that make sense and this is easiest if the overall structure of the presentation is made clear at the start. Even when individuals in the audience do not take notes, a clearly defined structure will help. Actually this is not as silly a predicament as the words suggest. A current debate in higher education research is whether or not students should be advised to take notes during a lecture. Many suggest that they should use the notes provided by the lecturer and to concentrate on listening rather than writing. For those interested in the debate on note taking I recommend online resources by Dhann (2001) and by Cottrell (2003). The latter reference does make the point that different lectures have different intended outcomes. Note taking (and design for note taking) may be more appropriate in some circumstances than in others. This certainly applies to presentations. Choosing the right structure to suit your intended outcome is important.

Another attribute associated with structure is 'the take-home message'. Most presentations do have one, perhaps two, really important messages or intended outcomes. Of course, this was considered above, under Content, but how the message is transferred from presenter to audience also relates to structure. The real message may appear at the beginning of the presentation, is then developed and supported in the middle, and summarized at the end. Or perhaps the message is slipped in at the end as it is only then that the audience will be prepared to understand it. These are considerations that relate to structure.

Beginning, middle and end

The simplest approach is to have a beginning, a middle and an end. The early part of the beginning is where you outline the story that you will tell. The latter part of the end is where you tell everyone where you have been. The middle part is where most of the content is. This is generally good for note taking. Audiences like this approach. I like this approach as it appeals to my need for order. Many, however, find it quite a dull approach, both for presentations and for story-telling. Those of you who have read Tolkien's *Lord of the Rings* trilogy will know what I mean – these books each tell several substories, cleverly interwoven to create one. I read these books with fascination, skipping backwards and sideways on occasions from section to section to check on events. The books are not printed in an entirely linear way, nor did I manage to read them in a linear way. There was no straightforward beginning, middle and end although it seemed that way on reaching the end, when the king married the elf princess and those that survived (mostly) lived happily ever after. But I would find it difficult to tell a story in a presentation like that; particularly in a short conference presentation.

If you do adopt a simple structure, you may benefit from some additional advice about how to structure your introduction. In general, an introduction should:

- describe what is known about your topic;
- identify what is not known about your topic;
- address what you have done about it (or will do about it).

In my experience, this level of structure and clarity always helps.

I have experienced other successful structures. One approach is to provide an interesting end point and then describe how you got there. Another is to provide several 'pieces of a jigsaw' and then fit them together. The mind map tools described in Chapter 3 offer one way of providing a 'whole story' graphic that can be dissected, bit by bit, but not necessarily in a linear fashion. As long as you carry the audience with you, then there is great scope for variation in structure. If you are in doubt though, please:

- tell them what you are going to tell them;
- then tell it to them, starting at the beginning and ending at the end;
- then tell them what you have told them.

Interaction with the audience

There are many ways to interact with your audience and most of these need to be designed into your presentation.

Eye contact

The importance of eye contact with the audience has been stressed in Chapter 2, alongside an analysis of its evidence base. Ignore this at your peril. Maintaining eye contact with as many individuals, and sections of the audience, as possible is the most important form of interaction that you can accomplish.

It is also fairly easy for most people to do as long as they think about it. It is all part of the process of decentring. You are there to talk with members of the audience. Explaining your topic is the most important thing for you to do and being sure that they understand what you are saying is all part of this. You cannot do this without looking at the expressions on the faces of the people that you are talking to. Most will agree that eyes can say a lot about how an individual feels. Wide disbelieving eyes are not a good sign. Eyes that glaze over with boredom or tiredness are similarly problematic for the presenter. Eyes that look at their watches or out of the window are even easier to interpret. We will consider this again in Chapter 5 when we discuss how you should prepare yourself for your presentation. Design your presentation around your need to decentre. The audience is important to you. Look at them.

Using examples relevant to your audience

It may be that your audience has chosen to be at your presentation because they know that you are talking about something that interests them. Lucky you. But sometimes it is not that straightforward and to really involve an audience you need to illustrate your talk with specific examples designed to grab their attention and make them feel that what you are saying has some link with their own experience.

Asking questions

This is a useful ploy to interact with your audience. Asking for a show of hands in response to a question near the start of your presentation will wake them up, make them feel involved, make them realize that you are indeed interested in what they think and may also provide you with important feedback on what their views are. There is a danger, however. If you ask a question that anticipates a response, but get no response, then it will undermine your confidence. You need to plan your questions carefully and plan how to get an answer. If you ask the whole audience a question that they can, as individuals, respond to with a show of hands then most will, eventually, do so. If the response required needs to be spoken, then most individuals will not speak if they can get away with it. One method is to move towards a specific person and ask that person, using eye contact to tell them that you expect an answer. Generally speaking you will get an answer in this way that you will then need to relay to the wider audience. Some might find this approach intimidating, but in my experience, as long as the approach is made in a friendly manner, it works for almost any audience.

Rhetorical questions also have their place but rarely involve the audience to the same degree as a real question.

Answering questions

It is important to establish some rules to regulate questions from the audience, unless these are already clear and taken for granted. If you allow questions during your presentation it will make the occasion appear less formal, but it plays havoc with your timing and may relinquish more control to the audience than you are happy with. Unless you are a confident speaker I advise you to ask the audience to leave their questions until after you finish speaking. In most conferences this is assumed to be the case unless otherwise indicated by the speaker or chairperson. Less formal seminars make up the rules as they go along but you should impose your own.

Then you need to consider how you will encourage questions. Questions, when you ask for them, are a form of feedback to you. For most presenters, there are few things worse than no questions at all. It might mean that you failed to put the audience at ease. Perhaps you bored them. Perhaps you confused them. Perhaps you performed so badly that the audience thought it kinder to just let you leave. Whatever the real feedback message, you will think all of these, and worse, apply to you if you leave the presentation having elicited no questions at all. Just one question is sometimes enough to give you that boost until the next time. To be sure that you get it you have to include that question in your design. Having designed the question in, you will be prepared to answer it.

You need to be one step ahead and think, 'if I were in that audience, what would I need to confirm or clarify at the end?' One approach is to avoid complete closure in your presentation. Leave something there that invites an audience to ask for more. We will consider how you can prepare yourself to answer questions in Chapter 5.

Moving around

I like to move around as I think it helps me to interact with the audience. I can look at, and talk with, specific groups in the audience if I am mobile. Sometimes this is difficult as you need to be near enough to the screen to point or because the room is just not designed for mobility. When I can, I do and I know that I move around too much for some people.

Giving a 'handout'

This is another excellent opportunity for interaction that is often wasted because the handout is provided before the presentation started or before the conference started! When you write your presentation you should be able to decide, by design, when a handout will be helpful to the audience and when the interaction will be helpful to you. Of course there is a scale factor here. Distributing a handout to a group of 20 in a small room is a different undertaking from doing the same for 200 in a large theatre.

Workshop tools

Staff developers have used a range of interactive devices in their workshops for many years to encourage participation, interaction and reflection. More recently, similar approaches have developed, particularly in higher education, to make lecturing to large groups more interactive. Techniques include dividing the large group into smaller groups and providing an activity that will lead to feedback to the larger group, or the introduction of a quiz or of a short debate. Some of these techniques may be suitable for some presentations. Although I use them routinely in staff development workshops and in my undergraduate teaching I had, until recently, not used them in a formal conference setting. I have seen them used to good effect but this does need a skilful and confident presenter. Indeed, most conferences related to learning and teaching in higher education use them routinely, but only sometimes successfully. There are many books in the higher education area about this. Gibbs, Habershaw and Habershaw (1984) have contributed *53 Interesting Things to Do in Your Lectures*, and Habershaw, Gibbs and Habershaw (1992) offer solutions to *53 Problems with Large Classes*.

Self-presentation

Figures 1.1 and 1.2 gave us an insight into what aspects of self-presentation are probably important, from the perspective of the audience. Actually, the list really focuses on those aspects of presentation that the audience was aware of. It is likely that we also make judgements about presenters, and people in general, that we are not overtly aware of. It seems that we have evolved as social animals to respond to all sorts of social events and circumstances automatically, without consciously thinking about it; more on this later.

The following comments were identified in Chapter 1.

Did not read from a script	She knew her subject well
Good use of English	Fluent speaker
She looked at the audience	It (she/he) seemed honest
She had a professional appearance	She looked relaxed
She was enthusiastic	She had charisma

So audiences like charismatic speakers that appear to know their subject well and do not read from a script, that speak fluent English, have a professional appearance and seem to be honest and relaxed. Easy! The point for this section of the book is that, with the exception of not reading from a script and using good English, these are all attributes of the presenter's appearance. She may have been a real fraud but she *appeared* to be honest. Whatever she said, and did, the audience interpreted it as honest and appreciated her presentation all the more for it. We do need to design this in, whatever this is!

Of course here we enter the world of non-verbal communication or body language. Not so much what we say, but how we say it and what we do while we are saying it. Some aspects of this will be addressed in depth in Chapter 5 when we consider how you should prepare yourself to present. Here we will attempt a broad coverage.

Non-verbal communication: is this science?

Many areas of science, and pseudo-science, converge to create huge general interest in this area but I am not personally totally convinced. Some highly reputable research comes from social psychology. I can recommend the works by Michael Argyle (1974), referenced also in Chapter 2. Another psychologist, Albert Mehrabian (1981) pioneered the understanding of non-verbal communication and established a classic statistic for the effectiveness of spoken communications:

7% of meaning is in the words that are spoken;
38% of meaning is in the way that the words are said; and
55% of meaning is in facial expression.

I am not qualified to judge how true this is or how effectively the work can be transferred to your presentation; but the figures are certainly thought provoking. Others are less circumspect about their doubts; one critic wrote an interesting article with the title 'Let's dump the 55%, 38%, 7% rule' (Oestreich, 1999). Another area of endeavour that contributes is that of ethology, the study of animal behaviour. Desmond Morris, author of *Primate Ethology* and the *Naked Ape* is an important name here. From a totally different direction, the work of Goleman (1997), on emotional intelligence, is relevant. Goleman considers our self-awareness, empathy and social-competence as elements of our emotional intelligence. Science or not, there is a huge public interest on how we communicate with or without words.

What parts of the body are involved?

From the above paragraph it is clear that facial expression is very important. These ideas are used to rationalize why telephone conversations are never quite as satisfactory as face-to-face conversations and why text-only communication seems doomed to failure. (Naturally things are never quite that straightforward. Texting and online chatting are clearly successful forms of communication for some, in some circumstances, for some purposes.) Our face, body, voice and hands all express emotions and help communicate interpersonal attitudes. They also work in conjunction with, and are synchronized to, verbal communication.

How can presenters benefit from knowledge about non-verbal communication?

Michael Argyle argues that senders and receivers may both be unaware of the various forms of non-verbal communication between them. Pupil dilation may be an example here; the sender is unaware that it is happening and the receiver is unaware that the communication is having an effect. For many other forms of non-verbal communication, the sender is unaware that communication is occurring but the receiver probably is. The majority of non-verbal communication fits this category. In both circumstances, however, Argyle suggests that training can help; senders can be helped to be aware of the signals being sent and receivers can be helped to interpret them.

   It is important to note that the precise meanings of non-verbal signals to the sender or to the receiver are not always clear. After all, senders and/or receivers may be unaware of what is happening. It is not a simple matter of asking them what they meant to say. Research does identify meaning but its further interpretation then depends on correct interpretation of research findings. Hence the disagreements and conjecture that plague this area of study. Here is an area of interest in which common sense does have to give way to experimentation and observation.

One example that relates to presentation: honesty

Chapter 5 looks at how you can prepare yourself to present and we shall consider the aspects of non-verbal communication that you should be aware of then. Meanwhile, let's consider one aspect of self-presentation that arose above. We shall look at body language and at the verbal language that contributes to an interpretation of honesty. Argyle identifies a range of behaviours that are interpreted by receivers as indicative of deception. He also describes a number of behaviours that tend to accompany deception. Slow speech, long pauses and raised pitch all signify deception. Interestingly, gaze aversion and speech errors are thought, by receivers, to indicate deception by the speaker, but probably do not (Argyle, 1988). The message for us, from the research, is that even if you are an honest presenter, you may inadvertently send out dishonesty signals.

However, I do wonder if we could actually get more clues, about how to come across as honest, from folklore than from social psychology. Walk tall, walk straight and look the world right in the eye. Avoid fast talkers and folk with shifty eyes. His voice said one thing but his eyes said another.

Presentation aids

General recommendations for visual aids are provided in Figure 4.2. Regular information about colour and complexity, and other features relevant to presentation aids are included in this table; but the table itself is not enough. Much of Chapter 3 concerns the issue of different individual and subject perspectives on how presentation aids should be used. Yet, here, in the chapter about design, I provide a catch-all visual. Even worse, the figure itself looks as if it could make a reasonable OHP transparency or projected PowerPoint slide but carries the label 'This page is far too busy to display on a screen, but it is probably fine as a handout'.

FIGURE 4.2

Guidelines for visual aids. This page is far too busy to display on a screen, but it is probably fine as a handout.

Guidelines for visual aids

5 to 7 double-spaced lines are generally acceptable
- Choose text and spacing to look good in the space available
- Choose a text-size in relation to the size of the room; it should all be readable
- Use bullet points for lists

Use colour with care
- Be consistent
- Look for good contrast
- White or yellow on a blue background is generally acceptable

Most audiences work best with charts and graphs
- The detail required is very discipline-dependent
- Avoid too much detail
- Avoid oversimplification

Choose fonts carefully
- Lower case is easier to read than upper case
- Arial and Tahoma are easy to read online
- Do not mix fonts

Printed text is easier to read than handwritten text
- Use the visual aid to add planned emphasis and punctuation to your verbal presentation

If you need to show numbers in a table
- Keep the data shown to a minimum
- Highlight really important data points

Some presenters in some disciplines ignore every aspect of this advice.

What are the key issues here? (in bullet-pointed clarity!):

- Most presenters in most situations would not attempt to provide so much detail on one slide; but some would and some of these could do this quite successfully.
- If this figure were to be converted into a slide, the text-size would be too small for most situations. Increasing the text-size would dramatically change its visual appearance.
- Each subsection has a few bullet points but each bullet point needs a substantial 'around the point' commentary. So for example, much more detail is provided below about the single bullet point 'Choose a text-size in relation to the size of the room; it should all be readable'. With this amount to say

about each bullet point, this one slide could support a 20-minute presentation. Most of us could find better ways to illustrate a 20-minute presentation than to use one poorly designed visual aid.

- The content is basically 'dull'; information that we all need to know but that no one wants to present as a long list or table. Instead, for example, several slides could be designed to illustrate good and bad points. These would probably support a presentation better than a long bullet-pointed list, but it would take a very good presenter to show them well in this way.
- If it is important that the audience has a record of each point, then the figure itself would make a good paper handout – that, after all, is what it is designed for.

Colours

Colours are important design features but unfortunately they are also subject to a range of individual preferences and accessibility issues. How you use colours to support your presentation is very much up to you, but how your audience perceives them is not.

Let's start with some of the accessibility issues. Colours are relevant to people with various forms of colour blindness and possibly also to people with dyslexia. The best source of information for us in this connection is from the various groups who specialize in designing learning resources for optimum accessibility. The UK source is TechDis (http://www.techdis.ac.uk/). Peter Rainger (2003) provides advice for preparing visual resources that are sympathetic to the needs of dyslexics. Draffan, Rainger and Corbett (2003) provide more generic advice that takes into account a range of colour-related visual factors. In general we are advised that high contrast between text and the background is more important than colour itself, but of course, the contrast that viewers see does depend on how their eyes and brain interpret the colours provided. So dark colours on a pale background are best. To maximize contrast, the background should not have any texture or pattern added. Particular combinations to avoid are red and black combinations; and red and green combinations. Some authors also suggest that black on white, while giving a high contrast, is a particular problem for some with scotopic sensitivity. My interpretation is that this applies particularly to high text densities, rather than to the low densities generally projected. If you are looking for a 'least-likely to cause problems solution' then the best advice is to use a combination of dark blue and creamy yellow. Rainger advises (for on-screen viewing) dark blue text on a cream background. Many others advise cream text on a mid blue background for projection. Personally I do prefer black text on a white background for some presentational material and I look with interest for further research in this area.

The one feature of generic advice that is consistently provided by all sources is to use colour consistently. It can be used to highlight important text as long as it is used consistently. It can be used to identify particular features in a presentation as long as it is internally consistent and consistent with codes anticipated by the audience. Red means 'stop' in western cultures and if we use it to indicate 'go' in our presentation then it will confuse. There is a general presumption that audiences prefer to use learning resources that contain some colour but there is little hard evidence that they learn better from coloured resources. Nor is there systematic evidence that these guidelines can be extrapolated between paper, the computer screen and onto projected images.

And then we really have to consider aesthetics. Lets face it, some colours go together and some do not. UK readers will be familiar with Lawrence Llewellyn-Bowen's take on interior design and may even be familiar with what is 'in' and what is not. But most of us have some colour sense that provides us with a reasonable guide and generally this does agree with the theory of colour. To do it technically we should use a colour wheel. Artists, flower arrangers and interior decorators use colour wheels, so why shouldn't we. It is possible to find these in books, but I always like to work from first principles. So let's try this as a mind experiment.

Picture a car tyre painted with the three primary colours, red, yellow and blue; each colour occupying about a third of the tyre. Now mix each colour with its neighbour to produce a block of orange (between the red and yellow), green (between the yellow and blue) and purple (between the blue and the red). We now have six colours on our tyre. Opposite colours are complementary; red and green, purple and yellow, blue and orange. Can you imagine these colour combinations together on a projected screen? If you paint your room with variants of these colours most people will think that the room looks all right. If you design your web pages along these lines, people might revisit them. The same applies to your presentation aids, with the added warning about the odd combinations in the previous paragraphs. One other bit of advice is to let your colours be subtle. I like the combination of purplish violet (the colour of heather flowers under a blue sky in late August before the frost gets them) against creamy yellow (the colour of cream on the top of proper milk after a warm day in the milk jug). (But I should add that my wife has never let me design colour combinations in our house since I matched sandalwood with accents of pillar-box red in the front room. Still, we learn from our mistakes. Perhaps that is why I tend to stick to black and white!).

If my mind experiment did not help you, I advise you to get a book from the local library. I am confident that Lawrence has written one.

Complexity

Figures 4.3 and 4.4 provide an example for us to use to discuss this issue. Figure 4.3 probably looks 'all right' to most people on the page. It was produced rapidly using Microsoft Excel. It contains some raw tabulated data; the number of people who collected at each of four sites on four occasions. It also contains a chart to provide a visual representation of how the numbers varied between occasions and locations. The whole figure is quite data-rich.

Figure 4.3, however, would not make a good projected visual aid for most of us. The text is too small and, in an average sized room with average projection, many people in the audience would not be able to read the numbers or distinguish between the data points on the graphic. To make it accessible we have to transform it into something like Figure 4.4. In Excel: I selected the chart; removed the grey background; increased the size of the markers (to 10 point) and changed them to maximize contrast with the background and themselves; removed the border and increased the line width of the axes; then changed the font size of all of the text to a minimum of 18 point. Figure 4.4 now only shows the graphical representation. It is still possible (perhaps even easier) to see how numbers have varied with location and occasion, and the text and markers are sufficiently large to show up just about anywhere, but some information has been lost to enable us to achieve this presentational clarity.

How acceptable this approach is depends on you and your audience. Some presenters do not worry that some of the audience cannot see the text and would prefer to use the original data-rich figure. I do worry about this and I will always sacrifice some content to ensure that it does not happen. Some

FIGURE 4.3

Was produced using Microsoft Excel. It contains raw tabulated data and a chart to provide a visual representation of how the numbers varied between occasions and locations. It would not make a good projected visual aid as much of the detail is too small.

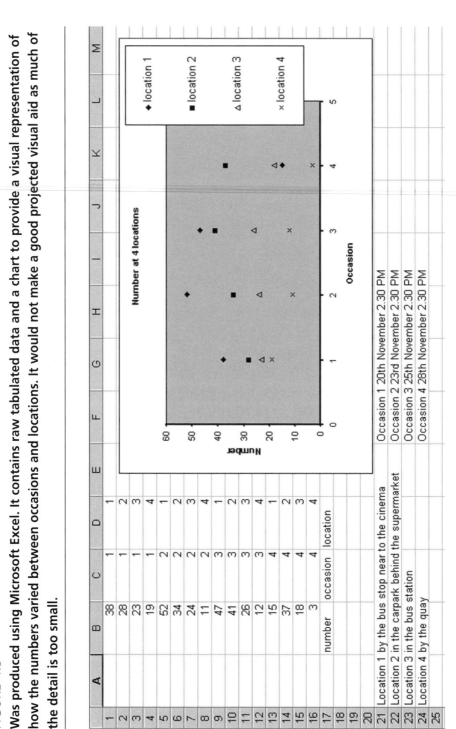

FIGURE 4.4

Consists of the same data as Figure 4.3 but shows only the chart reconstructed to produce a projected image with adequate text and symbol size.

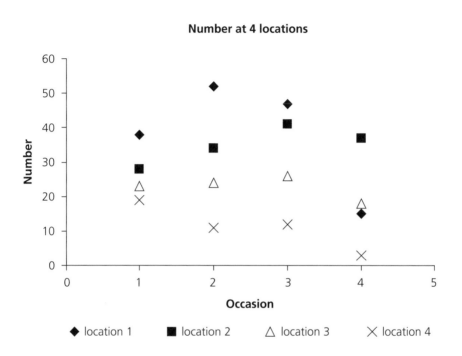

presenters would go further in this data-reducing direction. Some would not put these data points on the graphic and instead draw in a line to mark a trend. Personally I prefer to show the data points (my data always seems to have outliers that skew the means!). If I lose the data points because there are too many to show, then I want to add standard errors. I dislike showing only trends.

Data or graphs

If the audience expects to see original data and you show them a colourful pie chart or a simple line graph, then beware. If the data can be described algebraically and your audience is capable of interpreting this form of data representation then you need a good reason to take up time and space with a graph. This whole area equates strongly to audience expectations and your ability to anticipate and respond to these expectations.

Fonts and text size

You need to decide whose rulebook you will work to before you make decisions here. If you have as your founding principle (as I do) the notion that everyone in the audience must be able to see and read the captions to your figures, the numbers on your graph and all of the text, then you will want to follow the advice given in Chapter 3 about text-sizes for the OHP, for PowerPoint and for the whiteboard. You will probably have to resign yourself to producing clear, but rather dull, visual aids as well. If you are happy to liberate yourself from this constraint then you can carry on producing imaginative and visually appealing visual aids. I know that it is a tough decision. Some of the very best (visually-appealing) graphics that I have seen have been produced by engineers, but the detail on these fine images would not be readable to many in the audience. These clever people assure me that their audiences already know what the small text says, so they do not have to be able to read it. My audiences are never that predictable.

The choice of fonts requires a similar decision-making process. There is some evidence to suggest that fonts that work well on the page do not necessarily work well on the computer screen. I have not seen good data about extrapolating from the computer screen to the projected image but I think that we can work on the basis that this is possible. So, the fonts normally advised as suitable for both computer screens and projection are 'sans serif' fonts such as Arial (Helvetica), Verdana, Georgia, Tahoma and Trebuchet MS. These have clear, simple letter shapes, clear spacing between letter combinations and are easy to read. Much of the research in this area came about to help people with difficulties such as dyslexia. These fonts, however, turn out to be the most comfortable for most of us to read. Personal choice is also important. As I type this, I am using Times New Roman. I always do and I find it easy to read in books, on my computer screen and as a projected image. For my presentations, however, I routinely convert everything to Arial.

Audio and video

My next book may well be about using audio and video resources to support presentations and lectures; but here I have to confine myself to a paragraph. Several factors limit the use of these resources in presentations:

- The most important limitation is that they need 'technology'. A few years ago it would have been necessary to use a tape-recorder and speakers, a video cassette recorder or a film projector. Nowadays, audio and video can be based on a computer's hard disc, on a CD-ROM or streamed over the Internet. In all cases, however, the presenter has to acquire technological skills and rely on technology. Many choose not to.
- The second limitation has traditionally been the availability of resources. Nowadays, many more useful resources are available, particularly online. We are, after all, living in the information age. (Some sources are described in the bibliography.) Copyright issues are important, but if the resource is useful to your presentation (particularly to your audience) then it may well be worth the trouble to investigate the copyright situation. Whether you are into recordings of famous speeches, wildlife or wars, there is a lot of 'footage' out there to those prepared to look. But again, many choose not to.
- Tradition does limit the use of interesting and innovative resources. Tradition dictates that many presentations are oral presentations, not 'film shows' or 'slide shows'.
- Know-how also limits our use of these resources in presentations. Not my know-how or yours particularly; but that of the community of presenters in general. We are only now discovering how innovative use of multimedia resources can stimulate and support learning in higher education. This is new to many of us. The broadcasting and movie industry has been working on this for many years, but their focus has been entertainment and information. How we use such resources for motivating audiences to listen or to help explain difficult concepts is something new.

We have a lot of work in front of us before we catch up with what technology has made possible.

Backgrounds and design templates

The key point here is to avoid distracting your audience from what you are trying to communicate. If each slide that you show has a different design in the background then they may well be distracted away from your message. Over complex or highly coloured backgrounds may also be distracting, even if used consistently. Some people have seen so many PowerPoint presentations that they have grown to dislike the design templates that Microsoft provide. Indeed they dislike anything that looks like a Microsoft background. If your audience contains people like this, then it is probably not a good idea to use these templates!

I have, however, experienced good presentations that used visual aids with consistent, attractive backgrounds. Sometimes these use an information bar giving clues to the structure of the presentation. Sometimes they use a small and relevant image, in a corner or as a 'watermark'. There is lots of design potential here.

The logo

A logo is a combination of characters or graphics creating a single design and is generally used to identify a company. Personally, I do not like logo(s) on my slides. I feel that they occupy space that is desperately needed for my content. I also worry that they will distract attention from the points that I hope my slide will illustrate. So there, perhaps, is a guide for those of you who feel that you need to add your logo. Keep it small to reduce the space that it occupies and keep it consistent so that it distracts as little as possible. Make it transparent and I will be even happier.

Seriously though, some presenters do feel duty bound to show that they represent some body or that their work is owned by some particular corporation and you probably have no choice in the matter. Others feel that their presentation will be more credible if they give the impression that they represent some body or that some other group has a stake in their work. I cannot really argue with this either. If having a logo on your slides boosts your self-esteem and confidence, then use it.

However, I have seen some fairly impressive logos that add appeal to otherwise bland slides. The University of Southampton's dolphin is, I reluctantly agree, neat (check it out on www.soton.ac.uk) I know many academic presenters who are happy, even proud, to display the dolphin on their slides. I have also seen some awful logos that effectively dominate the whole design of the slide. Some pharmaceutical companies sponsor a lot of university research and clearly want everyone to know about it!

Copyright

Many sources could contribute useful presentation aids but are not easily available to us due to copyright restrictions. We have to take copyright seriously, if only because it is there to protect our interests as much as those of others. Many copyright owners are willing to grant permission for copyright-protected material to be used in presentation situations; but they have to be asked. Some copyright-protected materials automatically provide permission for such use in research and education settings. There are differences in how copyright-protected materials may be legitimately used between countries. In addition, authors of original work have moral rights, for example to be identified as the author or creator of the work, even if they do not hold its copyright. Particular issues do arise in relation to audio, video and image-based materials. This is a complex area and it will probably get more complex as the range of media diversifies and access improves with time. Sources of information on copyright are provided in the bibliography.

Is there room for individuality?

I think that there is. It may be that our own self-presentation is interpreted in rather fixed ways by the audience, based on the evolution of body language. I cannot argue about that. But interpretation of the design of our slides is less fixed. We have discussed subject differences in expectation and I think that there are also individual differences in expectation and appreciation. Perhaps we would not wish to doubt fundamental features of good design but I am confident that individuals in the audience will appreciate different things just as they do in the world of art and interior design. I like seeing good design but I also appreciate quirky design on occasions. Wouldn't it be dull if we all used presentation aids that looked the same, no matter how well designed?

Summary

This chapter addresses the elements of presentation design established in Chapter 1 as those most likely to separate good presentations from bad presentations. Content, structure, self-presentation, interaction and presentation aids are all important design features of your presentation that are themselves subject to the circumstances of your presentation and your own particular characteristics. This is a major design challenge for presenters but it is important to note that your own personal abilities have an overriding influence on the design of your presentation. How you prepare yourself is the topic of the next chapter.

References

Argyle, M. (1974) *The Psychology of Interpersonal Behaviour*, 2nd edn. Harmondsworth, UK: Penguin.

Argyle, M. (1988) *Bodily Communication,* 2nd edn. New York: Methuen.

Cottrell, S. (2003) Learning from lectures, http://www.palgrave.com/skills4study/html/learning_games/learningfromlectures.htm (accessed 27 January 2004).

Dhann, S. (2001) 'Note taking skills – from lectures and readings', http://www.ex.ac.uk/dll/studyskills/note_taking_skills.htm (accessed 27 January 2004).

Draffan, E.A. Rainger, P. and Corbett, R. (2003) 'Colour and contrast accessibility issues' (TechDis), http://www.techdis.ac.uk/seven/papers/.

Gibbs, G., Habershaw, S. and Habershaw, T. (1984) *53 Interesting Things to Do in Your Lectures.* Bristol: Technical and Educational Services.

Goleman, D. (1997) *Emotional Intelligence.* New York: Bantam Books.

Habershaw, S., Gibbs, G. and Habershaw, T. (1992) *53 Problems with Large Classes.* Bristol: Technical and Educational Services.

Mehrabian, A. (1981) *Silent Messages: Implicit Communication of Emotions and Attitudes.* Belmont, CA: Wadsworth.

Oestreich, H. (1999) 'Let's dump the 55%, 38%, 7% rule', *Transitions,* 7 (2): 11–14, http://www.cob.sjsu.edu/oestreich-h/Communic%20Article.doc (accessed 5 February 2004).

Rainger, P. (2003) 'A dyslexic perspective on e-content accessibility' (TechDis), http://www.techdis.ac.uk/seven/papers/ (accessed 27 January 2004).

Design concepts for new presenters

New presenters may be invited to present in a wide range of formats. Most of us are asked to deliver a poster, a departmental seminar or a short lecture first. Each has its own advantages and challenges. Designing the best presentation depends on what the audience expects, how nervous you are likely to be, how adventurous you are and what skills you have. If you are asked to speak in a language that is not your first, you have particular problems and responsibilities.

Your main design challenges can then be divided into;

■ *Content*: At a level and pace to suit the audience; and the title is important.
■ *Structure*: Something straightforward to start with, so that your audience knows where you are taking them.
■ *Interaction*: Many of the interactive elements so important to your presentation do need to be designed in. Use examples that the audience can relate to and design your presentation around your need to have eye contact with them.
■ *Self-presentation*: You need to consider not just what you say, but how you sound and look as well as what you do. Read about body language and consider how it might influence your presentation, but do not get too upset about this aspect of your presentation just yet. If this is your first presentation, you will have many more opportunities to experiment in the future.
■ *Presentation aids*: Having considered which to use, now you must design them. This is a big topic but I urge you to consider design from the perspective of your audience. Will your design match their expectations? Will the text be large enough for them to see? Will your aids actually help them?

5

Preparing Yourself

Key concepts in this chapter:

■ Prepare well and assess your confidence and self-esteem.

■ Rehearse to boost your confidence.

■ Benefit from supportive feedback.

■ Ensure that you are confident in your 'back-ups'.

■ Ensure that you are able to make eye contact with an audience.

■ Be prepared to answer questions.

■ Reflect on and practise your self-presentation.

In this chapter I will do my best to enable all potential presenters to confront their demons, overcome their problems and prepare themselves for their presentation. The problems of most presenters relate to being too nervous, having poor timing, unhelpful body language, poor self-esteem, lack of confidence and inadequate interaction with the audience. Many of these problems are made more severe by lack of personal preparation.

Prepare yourself: confidence and self-esteem

This section is partly about the effect of your nerves on your presentation. This is an odd prospect. The situation is entirely of your making. You chose to give the presentation. You designed the presentation. You prepared yourself for it. Yet here you are full of nerves about it. Colleagues who tell you 'being nervous is natural' are probably right, but are not necessarily helping you. They do not offer to give the presentation for you. They will not be standing in front of all those people. They do not have to remember the material and all of the nuances in delivery that you have had to practice. They won't have to face those awful questions. You will.

Actually, and logically, this is all about confidence. Presenters who are confident that they can do what they have said they will do may still have nerves, but they will not be debilitated by them. Nerves are natural but in a biological, evolutionary sense they are there to help you, not to debilitate you. Just think about it. Your big presentation is about to start. (*You have just spotted the giant antelope that you have been stalking for days*.) Blood drains from your face and hands, your stomach churns and you go pale and start to shake. (*You have just released adrenalin into your blood stream. This has redirected blood from your periphery and stomach to your brain and muscles, where it is most needed. Your blood sugar levels have risen and your senses are heightened. You are like a taught spring ready to launch your spear at your quarry*.) You suddenly have doubts that you can remember what to say first but you still step forward. (*You move towards the antelope, spear by your side, forcing your doubts away. If you fail now, your family will probably starve and the beast will impale you. Everything depends on you, but you can do it and you will do it*.) You move towards the lectern, acutely conscious of the audience, the chairperson and your presentation; almost as if this is not you, but someone else. You are in automatic mode. You know what you will do and this is your moment. (*The antelope raises his nostrils to the air; he has sensed you. He lets out a loud bellow and turns to run. You seize your moment and spring forward using your momentum to hurl your heavy spear into the animal's flank. He thrashes about in pain but you are on him, stabbing him in a frenzy of released tension*.)

Gripping stuff! Nerves are there to help you, but perhaps a little less of the frenzy will be helpful to allow your auto-start to develop into a more considered continuation of those first few moments.

So how do you build the confidence that you will need? How can you be sure that, when you step out in front of all of those people, you will not fail? Here are some suggestions:

- Work hard on the design of your presentation.
- Work hard on your presentation aids.
- Prepare back-ups of your presentation aids.
- Rehearse your presentation until you are happy with it.
- Practise your presentation in front of colleagues and ask them for constructive feedback.
- Rehearse it again after implementing aspects of the feedback that you like.
- Rehearse it again using your back-up presentation aids.
- Hope for the best but be prepared for the worst.

If all that sounds like hard work, that's because it is hard work. Be assured that there are many short cuts! Whether you take them or not will probably depend on two things:

1   How important is it that you actually present well?
2   Have you experienced failure before?

If the presentation is not that important, then you may be willing to risk failure and skip the rehearsals or the bit about feedback or practise with back-up presentation aids. You may get away with it. Most experienced presenters, however, can reflect on at least one important presentation where something went wrong. In my experience this is enough to change their views on shortcuts. There is probably a balance to be struck here. If you initially lack confidence then you need to go through the whole process to build confidence. If you are already filled with confidence then you will probably skip a few stages. There is one other factor that needs to be considered here. I tried to choose my words carefully at the start of this section: 'Presenters who are confident that they can do what they have said they will do … '. This is partly about confidence in general, but also about confidence in relation to a specific task. What did you say you would do? If you claim more authority on your topic than you can sustain, then you may feel vulnerable. You may respond by putting on a performance that will make you even more nervous. My advice is to make reasonable claims about what you can do; build up your confidence in your ability to do it and then to do it as well as you can. This advice is strongly supported by the literature. Argyle suggests that it is one way to reduce 'audience anxiety': 'If public speaker does not claim a self image which cannot be sustained, he is less vulnerable; whilst he must put on a performance, he can do it in a modest way' (Argyle, 1974: 207). The concept of status anxiety has developed further in recent years. There are apparently many of us who claim a status that is difficult to sustain (De Botton, 2004).

To recap: we considered the key aspects of the design of your presentation in Chapter 4. We looked at different types of presentation aid in Chapter 3 and at design principles for presentation aids in Chapter 4 again. We stressed the importance of the overhead projector as a back-up to more advanced visual aids in Chapter 3. Next we need to consider rehearsal and feedback.

Rehearse it until you are confident that it will work

Rehearsal seems to me to be an obvious and necessary aspect of self-preparation. When I started presenting at conferences I was rather shy. When a senior colleague suggested that I should rehearse in front of him, I was initially unwilling but eventually agreed. I am glad that I did, even though it was stressful, it enabled me to sort out some issues. At about the same time I discovered another important form of rehearsal. I had been trying to run through my presentation in my mind and I discovered that, no matter how many times I did, each time the presentation was different. It was too easy for my mind to wander. Almost in desperation I went for a walk alone around a large open space. I had my watch and I timed my presentation as I spoke it out aloud. This worked work well for me, for some reason, thinking about a presentation was not the same as speaking it. This accords with the views of Dance and Zac-Dance (1996). These authors recognize an internal spoken language and external spoken language. Our internal spoken language is silent, grammatically condensed and semantically condensed. You can handle thought much faster inside your mind than you can when it is linked to the spoken word. Rehearsal has to be out aloud for it to be effective.

Feedback

The issue of feedback is addressed in several locations in this book. Chapter 7 provides some pointers to feedback that relates to how you look and sound. Here I concentrate on feedback that relates to your presentation as well.

For this purpose you need feedback from an audience knowledgeable about the topic of your presentation. They need to follow what you are saying, or not, in the same way as the intended audience. They also need some particular characteristics. They need to be broadly supportive but confident enough about their relationship with you to be honest with you. They also have to have some empathy with the experiences that you are going through.

Having found the audience able to give feedback, you have to prepare them to give feedback and prepare yourself to listen to the feedback. Neither is easy. Ask them to give balanced feedback. Ask them to always tell you a mix of good things and bad things about your presentation. If they do not have anything good to say then you would be better not hearing anything from them! This is important because by the time you get to this stage you really need to be in a confidence-building phase. There are also other attributes of constructive feedback that can be important. Feedback ought to be specific ('It was all awful' will not help). Feedback should focus on behaviours that can be changed ('You were too short' will not help). Feedback that identifies some defect should, if at all possible, suggest an improvement ('I did not understand a key phrase that you spoke – could you write it on the board?'). Where possible, those who give feedback should label their own feelings rather than the actions of the presenter ('You were very arrogant' could be better expressed as 'You made me feel unimportant to you and I did not like that'). Giving feedback that obeys all of these guidelines is, however, quite a challenge; possibly too much of a challenge for a group inexperienced in the art of giving feedback. Balanced feedback is often as much as we can hope for.

To receive feedback you have to be receptive to it. No one likes criticism. I hate criticism. It always hurts a bit. But when the hurting stops you can step back and think about how to use the criticism to improve. At this stage a video recording of your rehearsal sometimes helps you interpret the feedback that colleagues can give. You might not realize how often you say 'um'. You do not really accept it when it appears in your feedback, but then you hear it for yourself.

Do not try to incorporate every aspect of feedback. You will not agree with some of it. Some of it may be helpful but require just too many changes to adopt in the time available. Some aspects of your presentation may be impossible to change in the short term. Take what is useful and usable and incorporate it.

I must add some words of warning about the power, and limitations, of feedback. There are three separate concerns that we must address. The first relates to your ability to cope with negative feedback. I said in a previous paragraph that it hurts. I did not say how much it can hurt. If you think that receiving negative feedback might be significantly damaging to you then you could start, say on your first rehearsal, by asking only for positive feedback. This will, hopefully boost your confidence a bit. Next time, with the benefit of this boost, and that of the initial rehearsal, you can ask each person to identify one thing only that could be improved. Be in charge. Be brave.

The second relates to the honesty of those giving feedback. When I first encountered dishonest feedback I was shocked. Now that I have encountered it on many occasions I am no longer shocked but I am uncertain about how to solve the problem. The dishonesty that I refer to is motivated by a desire to protect a presenter from an awful and embarrassing truth. Sometimes the presenter has a speech problem. Perhaps they say 'um' too often. The presenter with the 'um' problem asks a group of peers for feedback and all of them are too embarrassed to identify the 'ums' as a problem. They do not want to hurt the presenter's feelings. Very noble but not helpful. That same presenter will discover the problem in a less friendly environment at some later date. Another example relates to presenters whose first language is not English. Some really important words are mispronounced, resulting in the audience being confused and the presenter being frustrated. Feedback should identify the mispronounced word; but often it doesn't because, again, those giving feedback do not want to hurt the presenter's feelings. Actually one of these problems is worse than the other. The presenter with the 'um' problem will discover this if he records his practice presentation using video and watches it later. The presenter with the pronunciation problem will not necessarily benefit from this tool. I mentioned above that I am uncertain how to resolve this problem. Some people find it easy to give even the most 'cutting' feedback. Others are at the other extreme and seem unable to give even helpful feedback. This all has a strong affinity with the concepts of emotional intelligence (Goleman, 1997) and for those concerned about these things, the literature in this area could be useful. I am concerned and I have read a lot about it, but finding the right balance is a problem for most of us. My message for presenters is that you cannot totally rely on the honesty of those giving feedback.

The third limitation of feedback relates to the question of receiving feedback from people close to you, such as an employee, an employer, a close working colleague, or a partner. Some years ago I learned not to ask my wife to provide feedback on my professional activities. Even without my asking she tells me that I cannot teach, that I cannot explain even simple points and that I sound awful. (Bless her). It might all be true, and in the longer term I do have to address these issues, but it is certainly not balanced or overtly supportive. I have sought many other opportunities for feedback over the years that I have found more helpful. The point here is that it is unfair to ask people close to you for feedback on your presentation, because they will find it difficult to dissociate their views about you from those about your presentation skills.

Ensure that you are confident in your 'back-ups'

At the risk of labouring a point, I do want to stress again the importance of back-up strategies. This particularly applies to presentations that use presentation aids; and of these, to those that use high-tech aids. We examined the role of the low-tech overhead projector as a back-up presentation aid in Chapter 3. Here I want to stress how important it is to you that you are confident that these back-ups are ready to be used if necessary. In my experience, the effect of that spare copy of my presentation in my jacket pocket, on a floppy disc (or in my book, as a series of OHP transparencies or as a number of paper handouts) is immeasurable. Perhaps it is like an insurance policy, or like a good padlock on a bicycle. Once it is there you can stop worrying and get on with delivering your presentation. Forget it and you have to live with a nagging doubt that will erode your self-confidence.

Self-esteem

I think that self-esteem and confidence are different things. Presenters who prepare and rehearse adequately know that they will be able to present as planned. They have that confidence or feeling of certainty that they will succeed. It might be rough for a while but they will get there. To have self-esteem you need to go further than that. You have to have a sense of your own worth. I do not want to stray too far into the psychologists' domain but I do think that presenters need self-esteem before they can present well; perhaps before they can develop confidence in their ability to present.

So, how can presenters assess their own levels of self-esteem? And how can they boost these levels? I am not a lifestyle guru or a personality coach but this is my personal analysis.

In relation to the topics that I find myself presenting, and indeed in relation to the topic of this book, I get my self-esteem from study, research, engaging peers in discussion about the topic, writing for peer-reviewed journals and in general by being involved in the area. I think that I know enough about the topic to attempt to talk with others about it. I think that I probably know more about my little bit of the topic than anyone else, possibly in the world, and almost certainly than anyone in the audience. I may be deluding myself but I have self-esteem. I am worth listening to. I also have a well-prepared presentation and I am confident that I can deliver it. Of course self-esteem relates also to aspects of 'you' other than what you know about the topic of your presentation. Aspects of how you think you look are considered in Chapter 7 and some ideas of how you can improve your presentation style are considered in Chapter 9.

In my experience, most people who find themselves in the position of presenting at a conference or seminar do not lack self-esteem. They may lack confidence. If lack of self-esteem is your problem then I am not sure this book will help you. You need to know that you have something worth listening to!

Prepare yourself for interaction

Interacting with the audience is really important. You need to design interaction into your presentation, but you may also need to prepare yourself to interact.

Eye contact

Over the years I have come across many presenters who are quite capable of maintaining eye contact with the audience but forget to do so. I have also discovered a few who really find it difficult. They are also often the presenters who dread going to the conference most and those who most complain about lack of feedback from audiences. Bearing in mind that psychoanalysis is not my profession, I think that this is largely a confidence thing. So I ask people to try an experiment that at least identifies the extent of the problem. Try this: next time you walk down a corridor at work, rather than looking at the floor while you pass people, try looking at them. For the first few people that you pass, look at their feet. For the next few, look at their hands, then their shoulders, then their chins. Eventually pluck up the courage to look *briefly* at their eyes. When you have done this a few times return to this book and read on.

I am waiting for someone to tell me that it was a creepy experience and that I shouldn't have suggested it. Some report that they do this all the time and where else would your eyes look? Most tell me that it produced honest, friendly, human smiles on the faces of those encountered. I think that the same applies to conference presenters. Some stand at the front looking at anything but people's eyes; others stand there looking at me, you and at everyone else, drawing us all into the presentation using eye contact.

However, I need to add a couple of 'ifs' and 'buts' to this analysis. I stressed 'briefly' in the above experiment. Fleeting eye contact is generally appropriate. Longer eye contact many imply something beyond what you have in mind. You should also take into account cultural differences (described for example by McLaren, 1998) and gender differences (described by, for example, Argyle, 1988). It would be safest for me to advise you not to do anything that you are uncomfortable with; but perhaps an inability to make eye contact with the audience is related to a presenter's discomfort with the process. At least do the experiment in a safe working environment.

I guess that we all have our own styles of interacting with strangers. Perhaps mine is odd, but then again perhaps yours is too. I have a story to tell here that I think is relevant. One year, whilst visiting my parents in Surrey, a group of us went for an obligatory mid-morning walk. My sister-in-law-to-be joined us. As is my way when I am in a good mood, I greeted everyone that I encountered with a good morning or something like it. I noticed that sister-in-law-to-be gradually moved away from me. She eventually confided that, as far as she was concerned, only 'loonies' said good morning to people whilst on a walk in Surrey. Although I did not know it then, it is actually quite difficult to greet someone, particularly a stranger, unless you have made fleeting eye contact first. For some people, this level of interaction needs working at. You do not necessarily have to make eye contact with strangers in the street but, if you are to be able to do it with your audience, you should feel comfortable doing this around your workplace. I can

only provide a presentation perspective. Audiences generally respond well
to presenters who make eye contact with them.

Be prepared to answer questions

In Chapter 4 we discussed the importance of designing your presentation so that
it encourages the audience to ask questions and, indeed, to ask the right
questions at the right time. All this is possible through good design. Next you
do need to prepare yourself to answer the questions! But having designed the
question into your presentation, you should be able to answer it.

This should be part of your knowledge-base and present few problems to
you. Most of us, however, do have the experience of anticipating a question
and still managing to mess up the answer. Perhaps you give too long an
answer, or too detailed an answer for the audience and only managed to
confuse them more. Perhaps you responded in a know-it-all tone. The solution
is to prepare the answer as if it were an extension of your presentation. Do
not be afraid to revisit a particular slide, or even to have a slide in reserve
to illustrate the point that you are trying to emphasize. If all goes to plan,
the question and the answer should complement your conclusions rather
than confound them.

But what about the question that you had not anticipated? This is one of the
major fears that new academics have about the presentation – 'Perhaps there will
be someone in the audience who has it in for me and deliberately asks me an
awkward question'. Well, perhaps there will. Some sad people seem to go to
the conference for that reason only. But generally speaking, the question is not
as awful as you anticipate. If you cannot answer it, you should avoid pretending
that you can, and involve other members of the audience, for example: 'does
anyone else have more experience of that than I do?' This level of discussion is,
after all, what the occasion is for. Another solution is to say that you do not
know the answer but will attempt to find out more, later. You can even ask
to discuss the issue with the questioner over coffee. I did that once when a
questioner suggested that I had entered the research area 'with both feet off
the ground' as I hadn't read a vital reference. (I guess that the criticism was just,
but the reference was very old and I found the discussion over coffee to be
non-illuminating.) Never, ever respond to a nasty question with a nasty answer.

In my experience, the audience will always recognize a nasty question and will respect you for your professional response. Prepare yourself by thinking about the full range of difficult questions that you might be asked, and practise two or three suitable responses.

When I started delivering papers at conferences I went through a phase of being quite confident about my ability to answer questions. I suspect now that my responses sounded smug. I am less confident now. Perhaps my brain is slowing. Perhaps I am talking about more complex problems nowadays. Or perhaps I am just less smug than I used to be.

Prepare your self-presentation

In Chapter 4 we considered how presenters may send out signals to the audience without being aware that they are doing so. Part of your preparation could be to identify these signals and to correct them when they are inappropriate and when it is possible and desirable to do so. However, this section comes with a 'Kerry's health warning'. To some extent you are what you are. Perhaps you do inadvertently deliver the 'wrong' signals; well, that is how people normally see you. You are being honest about yourself and not pretending to be someone else or something that you are not. Perhaps a rule of thumb should be that you should 'stay yourself' unless significant feedback informs you that others see you as a person that you don't want to be. There may be a particular mannerism that you have that you want to get rid off. But there will be a cost. Not only will you have to make an effort to change but you may find that effort, combined with the nervousness you may experience when delivering a presentation, will be too much. Remember that audiences appreciate honesty, or at least the appearance of honesty. If you have to make such an effort to change your body language, so that you then come across as dishonest, this will not help you.

As described in Chapter 4, some aspects of body language are not intuitive and we understand them, to a degree, only as a result of careful observation and research. We shall focus here on aspects commonly reported as contributing to good presentations, reviewed in Chapter 1 and inverted here to indicate what to avoid. The analysis then describes aspects of body language that can be involved. Much is based on the work of Argyle (1988).

Not looking relaxed

It is possible that audiences, faced with a presenter who looks relaxed, think that she knows her subject, is well prepared and has authority. People show relaxation particularly in their posture. Psychologists suggest that, to a degree, a relaxed posture suggests dominance. Too much relaxation, however, suggests dislike.

Lacking enthusiasm

Enthusiastic presenters raise the pitch of their voice to give emphasis. They also raise eyebrows, hands and shoulders and smile a lot.

Lacking charisma

I do not know which elements of body language contribute to charisma. No one has ever included this complement in feedback to me. Charm, yes (as described in Chapter 7); charisma, no. Wainwright (1985) does provide an analysis of key aspects of body language that contribute to charisma and adds to this an analysis of how to be more attractive. Good luck!

Appearing to be dishonest

This was addressed in Chapter 4 where I suggested that unduly slow speech, long pauses and raised pitch might all signify deception in some circumstances. Gaze aversion and speech errors may also be interpreted as indicative of speaker-deception. If you are honest and you want to appear to be honest then I suggest you should attempt to speak at a reasonable pace, avoid long pauses and look at the people in your audience.

Not engaging with the audience from the start

Paraphrase this to 'stand-off-ish' or 'distant' or 'non-communicative' and then we are in the realm of bodily communication. People tend to stand closer to others that they like and they lean towards them, rather than away from them. Engaging presenters will spend as little time as possible looking away from their audience, at notes or at the screen. Engaging presenters will also use hand gestures for emphasis or to gain and maintain audience attention. They often have open arms and exposed palms. They will also use non-verbal signals consistently and synchronized with verbal messages. A speaker who steps backwards at the same time as making positive, inclusive verbal comments is likely to be interpreted negatively no matter how positive the words are.

Having an unprofessional appearance

This relates primarily to what presenters wear, although aspects of personal appearance such as hairstyle may be important. Often people will come to your presentation not knowing what you look like. They will have a name and possibly some idea of your reputation. Perhaps they will already have an image in their own minds of what you look like. If you disappoint them then you are probably starting at a disadvantage.

Every profession exerts some pressure on individuals to conform to certain situation norms. In addition, as individuals we tend to use clothes to express our personality. Psychologists tell us that we also choose the way that we wear our clothes as a form of communication. People tend to respond best to those with similar appearances to themselves so all of these factors can be used to encourage positive responses from the audience.

In some respects, therefore, we can influence the response that we get from the audience by choosing appropriate or inappropriate clothes; but only if we know the audience well enough. I tend not to wear a tie at work nowadays and at most conferences I also spend most time without a tie on. I generally do not wear a tie for a departmental seminar or for many other less formal occasions. I do, however, always wear a tie for a formal conference presentation. Having said that, if my friends thought that I was giving fashion advice to anyone they would be highly amused!

Summary

Preparing yourself to present makes a huge contribution to successful presentation. This chapter makes specific recommendations about how you can prepare yourself to interact with your audience and to prepare your self-presentation. Building your own confidence in your ability to present by sound preparation, adequate rehearsal and useful feedback are all important elements of this process. Next we have to look at what you can do to ensure that your presentation venue is adequately prepared for you.

References

Argyle, M. (1974) *The Psychology of Interpersonal Behaviour,* 2nd edn. Harmondsworth, UK: Penguin.

Argyle, M. (1988) *Bodily Communication,* 2nd edn. New York: Methuen.

Dance, F.E.X. and Zac-Dance, C.C. (1996) *Speaking your Mind: Private Thinking and Public Speaking,* 2nd edn. Dubuque, IA: Kendall/Hunt.

De Botton, A. (2004) *Status Anxiety.* New York: Pantheon Books.

Goleman, D. (1997) *Emotional Intelligence.* New York: Bantam Books.

McLaren, M.C. (1998) *Interpreting Cultural Differences: The Challenge of Intercultural Communication.* Dereham, Norfolk, UK: Peter Francis Publishers.

Wainwright, G.R. (1985) *Body Language.* Sevenoaks, UK: Hodder and Stoughton.

How new presenters can prepare themselves for presentation

If this is a high-stakes first presentation, then you will want to leave as little to chance as possible. Rehearsal and supportive feedback will boost your confidence as well as help you to acquire skills in presentation. Therefore, you need to:

- Work hard on the design of your presentation.
- Work hard on your presentation aids.
- Prepare back-ups of your presentation aids.
- Rehearse your presentation until you are happy with it.
- Practise your presentation in front of friends and ask them for constructive feedback.
- Rehearse it again after implementing aspects of the feedback that you like.
- Rehearse it again using your back-up presentation aids.

Whilst rehearsing:

- Ensure that you are able to make eye contact with an audience.
- Be prepared to answer questions.
- Reflect on and practise your self-presentation.

6

Preparations Specific to the Venue

Key concepts in this chapter:

■ What you need to know about the venue.

■ What the venue needs to know about you.

■ How to organize your presentation aids.

■ How to be sure that you will get there.

■ Coping with lights, wires, new computers, pointers and projectors.

■ Be sure about your back-ups.

I am sure that everybody who has ever been to a conference or to a large meeting will have experienced disasters that occurred because somebody made a mistake. Most often it is someone else's fault, of course. They didn't show the presenter where the light switches were. They lost the presenter's presentation aids. They didn't check that the presenter's version of PowerPoint was the same as the version available on the presentation computer. It wasn't possible to turn the lights low enough for the audience to see the slides. They forgot to tell the presenter that the presentation slot was 20 minutes, not 30 minutes. Someone else's fault. But the major theme in this chapter is that, as a presenter, you cannot blame other people. The main reason for this is that the audience is unlikely to blame other people. They are sitting there waiting for you to present something and you don't manage to. They won't blame the institution for not fitting blinds to the windows. They won't blame the technicians or the organizers for all sorts of problems; they will blame you. So my message here is that you have to cover the tracks of others. Others may say that it is their role to do this or that, but it is your role to ensure that the deed is done.

I will emphasize the notion of responsibility by using a case study. Here is an example where a number of presenters didn't think about how to ensure that the venue for their presentation was suitable for them and for their audience. In some ways this is an example of a failure to decentre; a failure to think about how the audience will see a particular presentation. Presenters who think about their audience will want to arrange the venue so that the needs of the audience are satisfied. I don't think this comes naturally to new presenters. Indeed, I suspect the process of decentring is not an easy attribute to acquire. It takes experience and sometimes it takes bad experiences. Here is one that I was at least partly responsible for!

CASE STUDY 6.1
New lecturers struggle with cardboard boxes

One of my roles is to help facilitate aspects of our 'New Lecturers Workshop'. In this event, staff new to lecturing meet in small groups to practise their lecturing style and give each other feedback. My role as facilitator is to enable these interactions to occur and to support the feedback process. There is much in common between these workshops and those described for presenters, in Chapter 1.

On this occasion we had to work in a room new to us. The room was a lecture room in that it had a whiteboard and desks but it was also used for storage. There were piles of cardboard boxes dotted around the room including one stack of boxes under the whiteboard. I did not notice this stack until it was too late as I was working at the back of the room with the camera. As always, I advised the participants to ensure that the room was arranged to suit what they would be doing. Most participants were to use the overhead projector and started by arranging this properly. Some were to use the whiteboard and they checked that it was cleaned and that the pens worked.

The next hour was occupied by six short consecutive lectures. Most of these made use of the whiteboard. All lecturers struggled around the cardboard boxes. Short lecturers found they couldn't reach the top of the board because of the boxes. Even tall lecturers had problems. They had to stand right in front of the boxes to write, so obstructing the audience's view of the board. Interestingly, the audience picked up on the problem after the first lecture. But none of the lecturers, who made up the audience, did anything about the boxes before they gave their own lecture. Everyone chose to work around the boxes even after they realized that this was disruptive for them and potentially for the audience. This was particularly obvious in the video playback of the short lectures.

I am confident that these new lecturers learned a valuable lesson in this workshop. Perhaps initially some blamed me for not moving the boxes; but after seeing the video recordings and reflecting on matters as a group they identified the problem as theirs. I am confident that these new lecturers will remove cardboard boxes from wherever they teach in the future. (Perhaps I should always plant cardboard boxes in front of all whiteboards where this workshop occurs!) The message for us, however, is that we must prepare our venue to suit our own presentation, and not rely on others to do this for us.

In the weeks before the presentation

What do you need to know about the venue?

You need to know a lot of information about the venue. The more you know, the better you will be able to prepare yourself for the venue *and the venue for you*. In terms of preparing the venue for you, you will need to discuss your specific requirements with the organizer and possibly with the IT technician. Perhaps a particular item of software will be necessary for your presentation to run. Will they let you load it onto the presentation computer yourself? If so, when? Should you bring your own laptop? In particular, you need to know the following:

- How large the room will be.
- How many people there will be there.
- Who these people are.
- What else is occurring around your presentation. Which other presentations? Who are the other presenters?
- What audio-visual facilities will be present. Which version of Microsoft Office will be loaded onto the computer? Which versions of Internet Explorer or Netscape? Will you have access to the room before your presentation? Will the computer have Internet access? Will there be an IT technician available? Can you contact her?
- Who will be chairing the meeting. You may wish to ensure that they have enough information about you to properly introduce you.
- Exactly where the venue is. Not just the institution. You need a full postal address and if possible the name and number of the building and room that the presentation will occur in. Most institutions provide online maps that are a great asset to presenters.

What does the venue need from you?

Generally the organizers need you to tell them as much as possible. There are many books on organizing meetings and conferences but the work involved has to be experienced to be believed. A well-respected guide was originally produced by Seekings (1981). Seekings advises conference planners to adopt the principle that speakers must be told everything that they need to know and leave nothing to chance. Good event organizers will tell presenters everything in my list above (What do you need to know about the venue?), without you having to ask. I do wish that more events organizers would read Seekings.

My own experience of the task of organizing conferences and meetings is that someone must check that everything that should be done is done; otherwise it might not be. If something is not one person's responsibility then the chances are that it will not be done properly. This applies in particular to organizing presenters. My own experience of being a presenter is that event organizers often do not manage to cover everything and that it is vital that presenters do not assume that they will. If planners adopt Seekings' advice and presenters adopt my advice there will, at least, be plenty of information flowing.

Organizers will probably need:

- the title of your presentation;
- a summary or abstract;
- some information about your career so far;
- a list of any specific requirements such as software.

As a presenter, you can help the organizers by:

- submitting your information on time;
- avoiding, at all costs, subsequent changes;
- being as straightforward in your needs as possible.

(I generally fall down on the last point. I always seem to need some particular presentations aid or software.)

This book is not about the broader conference experience but many presentations are reproduced as a paper in a publication of conference proceedings. Preparations for this activity often accompany those for the presentation itself. Publishing conference proceedings brings with it a host of additional organizational pitfalls. You can help the organizers by responding properly to their requests for documents; on their terms, to their deadlines and using their suggested formats. It is a difficult job and they need all the help that you can provide.

Organizing your presentation aids

There are many possibilities here. I probably tend to go 'over the top'. I like to check everything and perhaps I sometimes make a nuisance of myself before the presentation. But this gives me more confidence that everything will work during the presentation.

Perhaps most obviously you should ensure that everything works at your own institution or in your own office before you go. Check it out on your own overhead projector. Ensure that it works on your own computer. Of course it will. You will have undertaken all of the rehearsal activities recommended in Chapter 5.

The next stage is to see if you can get your presentation aids to the venue before the event. Many large conferences provide a facility where you can e-mail your PowerPoint presentation to an IT technician before the conference. In theory your presentation will therefore be loaded onto the presentation computer before you arrive. Again in theory, the IT technician would have checked that your presentation works in its new environment. Even in smaller scale events, it may be possible to send presentation aids in advance. For departmental seminars this often proves possible and is also appreciated. Many departments in modern universities are taking presentation aids very seriously. Some businesses are even better provided with technical support and it is good to involve these people in presentations if at all possible.

How will you get there?

Deciding how you will get to your presentation is often a huge challenge and your decision depends very much on how high the stakes are. If this is an important presentation and you do not want to leave anything to chance, then you really have to travel the day before. I always dread conference presentations where I am to present in the morning of the first day. This often means travelling on a Sunday, resulting in family upsets and dependence on substandard public transport (engineering work always tends to disrupt the rail network on Sundays), followed by a lonely evening meal in an awful student residence in the middle of nowhere. But if the presentation is important then you might have to do it. Perhaps the conference is in a posh hotel, in which case the balance tips a little more in favour of travelling the day before! Yes I do drive sometimes, but often travelling on modern motorways is as unreliable as on trains – it is quite possible to be stuck in a motorway jam for three hours or more.

But where do you draw the line? Should you travel the day before to a departmental seminar at a university 50 miles away? Probably not, but you should try to leave some hours in reserve; enough to cope with unexpected road works, running out of petrol or minor accidents. As I write this I know that I have to present at a workshop tomorrow at 10.00 at a university 60 miles away. It generally takes 90 minutes to drive there but I will be travelling in the rush hour and I need at least 30 minutes to prepare when I get there. Therefore, I aim to leave home at 06.45, and I will ensure that the car is full of petrol this evening.

What about the research team presentation at your normal place of work? My advice would be to stick to your normal routine, particularly if you normally get to work at about the same time each day and if your presentation is not scheduled for 09.00.

On the day of the presentation

You must attempt to gain access to the room in which your presentation will occur as far in advance of the presentation as possible. You have a lot to do.

Lighting and sound

You need to check that you can control the lighting in the presentation room. Some lecture theatres have complex controls. How organizers expect presenters to know how these work is beyond me. Most universities do run staff training sessions on how these controls work and very few lecturers ever go to them. Training is generally by trial-and-error. You have to go and check the controls out for yourself. If the system is complex, it is worthwhile making brief notes or even a small diagram, just to remind you which button does the important functions.

If you intend to use audio-visual aids, other than those operated by a computer that you are familiar with, then you may need the help of a local technical support person. This must be organized in advance.

Even with all of these preparations, things can still go wrong. At my last major presentation, the chairperson for my session did not turn up and the room was occupied by an impromptu presentation, at the time that I, and others, had prearranged to load our presentation aids. When these things happen, only your own personal preparation and resourcefulness will get you through. Perhaps a bit of luck helps; but if I had been lucky these events would not have occurred in the first place. Luck has very little to do with it.

Wires and other obstacles

As I have described in other chapters, I like to move around while I am giving a presentation. I also move my hands quite a lot. So, I need to be sure that I am not going to trip over something or knock something over. I can do this by going into the room before the presentation to check it out. I move things that could easily be knocked over. I make a mental note of where cables lie on the floor. I move unwanted objects to one side (not too far in case another presenter wants them!). In some conferences, this pre-session activity can be quite a social gathering.

Organizing your presentation aids

If you didn't get your presentation aids loaded onto the computer before the conference then you should do it now. You need this opportunity to test that it all works as you think it should. If it doesn't then you need time to fix it. If you have been told that you can use your own laptop, try it now. This particularly applies if you need to access the Internet during your presentation. You will not have time either before or during your presentation to undertake complex reconfiguration, but this will not be necessary if the host institution's IP addresses are dynamically allocated. But do not take someone's word for this, test it yourself.

Another task at this stage is to organize your pointer. If you are to use the OHP then this is straightforward. You can use a pencil to point to detail on the OHP itself. If you use slides or a computer then the situation is more complex. Personally I like to stand in front of the screen and point with my hand. This works for me but only if the screen is low enough. Often it is not and on more than one occasion I have found myself jumping to reach detail on a screen 3 metres up. I am sure that the audience were amused but I felt silly. I have seen other speakers who were not willing to expose themselves to ridicule in this way and preferred to wave in the general direction of the screen even if this meant that the audience could not identify the point in question. Find a pointer and practise with it. Is there a long stick in the corner? What about a laser pointer? If this is a proper conference then there should be a laser pointer available. Many experienced presenters are wise to this problem and take their own laser pointer!

Controlling the technology

One of the commonest disasters is that organizers of presentations arrange for a presentation computer that has an inbuilt 'mouse'. Mouse is probably the wrong word as most of these computers have strange devices that theoretically, and with a great deal of practice, allow the user to move the cursor over the screen. In practice, presenters always struggle to use these devices to control their presentation. Cursors fly around the screen to the amusement of the audience and the frustration of the presenter. I always ask organizers to ensure that presentation computers have a conventional mouse attached.

Some don't like it. In that case I bring my own mouse and connect it to the computer before my presentation, as I cannot use mouse-like appendages on strange computers.

Organizing your 'back-up'

I hope that you got the message in earlier chapters that your back-up presentation aids are as important as the real thing. When you check the room's computer spend a few minutes looking at the whiteboard and flip chart. (Are the pens available? Is there a board wiper?) And what about the overhead projector? Where is it? How long will it take to bring it into action? Can you switch it on and off? Is there somewhere near it to place your pile of transparencies? What about your written notes? If your brain does stop working, these are the back-ups that you will resort to. Will they work for you?

Seating arrangements

It may be that you have no control over seating. In a large conference setting this will certainly be the case. But if your presentation is a smaller departmental seminar or a research group meeting then you may have some control. Seating arrangements make a big difference to how you can interact with your audience. Here are some suggestions;

- Everyone in the room needs to be able to see you and any presentation aid that you use.
- For small groups, try to arrange chairs so that everyone is in the front row.
- If you need more rows they should be staggered to enable people to see between the people in the row in front.
- You can encourage interaction and discussion for a meeting, by generating a 'round table' arrangement.
- For small group presentations, the ideal is to be as near to members of the audience as they are to each other.
- If there are more chairs than people, some groups have a tendency to sit at the back. You can ask them to move forward, but an effective plan is to remove some chairs from the front rows to give you walking access to people further back.

Summary

This chapter described how to ensure that your hosts know about your needs and that you provide enough information for their needs. It looked at the preparation of your presentation aids and last minute activities in your presentation room.

For many, this is a watershed chapter. All of your key preparations have been completed. You have prepared your presentation, yourself and venue-specific activities that are open to your intervention. You should now be ready to present. Chapter 7 is about videoconferencing. Chapter 8 is about last-minute checks and mid-presentation disaster recovery. Chapter 9 is about long-term improvement strategies. All plain-sailing from now on!

Reference

Seekings, D. (1981) *How to Organise Effective Conferences and Meetings*. London: Kogan Page.

How new presenters can prepare their venue for their presentation

If you thought that all you had to do was turn up and present, you must think again. Many problems are caused by lack of 'last-minute preparation' or by assuming that others will do things that they say they will do.

- Find out as much as you can about your presentation venue – where it is, how large the room is, what equipment it has, and much, much, more besides. Write a list of questions for the organizers.
- Ensure that the organizers know as much about you, and your presentation, as possible. Communication is vital, do not leave this to others if you can help it.

∎ Plan your travel arrangements meticulously.
∎ On the day of the presentation, ensure that you gain access to the presentation room to gain familiarity with the equipment, test your presentation aids, and if possible ensure that you are happy with the seating arrangement.
∎ Organize how you will implement your back-up plans.

7

Videoconferencing

Key concepts in this chapter:

▮ Presentations over a video-link can be very good.

▮ Videoconferences (VCs) can be one-to-one, one-to-many, several-to-several or several-to-many.

▮ How to cope with the camera and microphone.

▮ Using feedback to give you confidence in the way you look and sound.

▮ You need to practise using the technology.

▮ Preparing to control complex interactions.

▮ How to be seen and heard in group-to-group videoconferences.

▮ Background information on videoconferencing technology.

Have you ever been invited to give a presentation at a conference (perhaps to give a keynote address) but been too busy to actually go, and then find that the conference organizers are so keen to have you that they suggest a video-link to bring you in *virtually*. Wow, you must be an important person in your field. No, it doesn't happen in this way to all of us! But many of us will be, or have already been, involved in some way in a videoconference.

When it does happen the results can be very good. I have attended conferences in the UK where a keynote presenter delivered presentations live over a video-link from her office on the other side of the world. On one occasion the audience saw the presenter's slides in a PowerPoint presentation. They also saw a still image of the presenter and benefited from an excellent audio-link. The audience asked questions via a roving microphone and received good spoken answers. On another occasion the audience could see a good-sized head and shoulders real-time image of the presenter as well as hear his voice and see his slides. It takes some organization and lots of technology but it can be done. (Of course this leaves aside the issue of whether it should be done!). More recently I have 'attended' web-casts (like broadcasts but over the web) where a presenter, or often a team of presenters, have given presentations that have been seen, heard and interacted with by participants all over the world, each sitting at their own computer, as individuals or in small groups. The range of media used to support these presentations is impressive and, often, the experience of participants is really good. I have been part of multiple group videoconferences on many occasions, often to discuss the development of research projects. I have even presented to an academic conference over a video-link; unfortunately not as a keynote speaker but as described in the case study in this chapter.

Videoconferencing is here to stay and it is getting better all the time. It is also quite variable in its operation and it is worthwhile considering this as it has a bearing on how the presenter is seen, how he or she should prepare and what can be achieved.

Generally the main aim in conducting a videoconference is to save on travel time and expense for the presenter and increasingly for the audience. Often videoconferencing allows interactions to occur that simply would not occur if presenters and audiences had to travel. This has to be a good use for technology; to enable things to happen that could or would not happen without it. If only all uses of technologies were this rational!

How technical do you want this?

If you need to know how it all works then you should read the texts included in the References at the end of the chapter, but be warned that the technology changes at a fast pace.

If you want to know enough about the technology and terminology to be able to communicate intelligently with the IT technicians who will contact you from the conference's host institution, then you had better familiarize yourself with the terminology provided in the section 'Some background information on videoconferencing technology' towards the end of this chapter.

If you just need to know how it will influence you, as a presenter, then read on here.

Basics of the videoconference

The standard approach to categorizing videoconferences is to describe them as:

- One-to-one: where two individuals or groups exchange audio and video with each other on a one-to-one basis.
- One-to-many: where one individual or group can be seen and heard by many individuals or groups.
- Several-to-several: where several groups or individuals communicate with each other.
- Several-to-many: where the output of a group of videoconferencing systems can be seen and heard by many receiving systems.

This categorization is important for those planning and establishing videoconferences, as it describes the type and complexity of the technologies involved. It is also worthwhile becoming familiar with the concepts involved, as they will be around for a while. But presenters are generally more interested in a range of fairly basic operational factors that directly influence what they can do and how they need to prepare. These include the following:

- To what extent will the 'audience' be able to interact with me? They will see and hear me, but will I be able to see and hear them? Will they be able to ask me questions? Will I be able to get feedback from them? Can the interaction be 'talking with our voices' or will we have to 'chat' by typing?
- What audio-visual aids will I be able to use? Can I show PowerPoint slides or video clips? How much control will I have over these media at the other end?
- What new skills will I need? Will I need to learn new IT techniques or how to work new software? Will my normal presentation skills work in front of a camera? Will the technology place particular demands on me? How will I be able to evaluate my own 'performance'?

These are all very reasonable concerns for those about to confront videoconferencing. In general they are not just technology concerns, as they relate to the craft of the presenter. My approach to answering these questions is to describe a number of scenarios, each progressively more complicated. Where key issues are identified, then these are brought out in more detail.

Key issues for simple one-way or limited feedback videoconferencing include:

- camera, microphone and interview craft;
- feedback and evaluation;
- practice.

For web-casts, virtual learning environments and live lectures at a distance, key issues are:

- controlling complex resources;
- controlling complex interaction.

And with group-to-group videoconferencing, a key issue is how to be seen and heard.

As this is just one chapter within a book about presenting at conferences, I concentrate here on aspects of presenting that relate to videoconferences in particular. Aspects of *what* you say are the topics of other chapters. In this chapter we are most concerned about what you look and sound like and what control you have over this.

Simple presentations in a videoconference environment

The simplest systems are often primarily 'one-way'. You sit in front of a camera and microphone in Bognor Regis and your image and voice is relayed to an audience in Hawaii via a video projector and loudspeaker. This is just like being live on television. You cannot see or hear the audience. Or you may have, just as effectively, recorded your presentation. If it really is one-way transmission then the audience will not know, and neither will you!

Your signals could be transmitted via a dedicated telephone line or lines using specialized equipment, or via the Internet, perhaps with a simple modem connection. The camera might be a sophisticated television camera or a simple webcam sitting on the top of your computer. You might be just reading or speaking but you might be using a PowerPoint presentation via requests to the IT technician or chairperson at the other end for the 'next slide please'.

In my experience the key issue for you, the distance presenter, is that you get no feedback from the audience. They may have fallen asleep or left. Of course this is the same as making a live broadcast. No one may be watching!

Key issue: camera, microphone and interview craft

You should not be in doubt that there are particular skills involved in talking into a microphone in front of a camera. We do not all naturally look and sound good in these circumstances. Some of us look really silly and sound terrible. Some of us actually do look good to viewers but not to ourselves. Some of us look at the ground. Some of us twitch. Some of us say 'um' between every other word. To an extent, acting on the advice and instructions of an interviewer can compensate for our natural deficiencies. A good interviewer will tell you where to stand and pick up on your most obvious problems. That is at least part of the interviewer's role. But in many videoconferencing applications there is no interviewer; just you, the microphone, the camera; and the rest of the world looking at you.

In the mid-1990s I attended a media skills course run by Hillside Studios in the UK. The course was designed to prepare people for radio and television presentation but much of it is relevant to the videoconference presenter. The tutors provided participants with preparatory tasks before the course. We had to prepare short interview 'scripts' and prepare briefing material for the tutors on the topic. We took turns to give 3-minute radio interviews, 3-minute television interviews and 2-minute 'down the line interviews'. (This is where the interviewer is in one studio and the presenter in another, a situation most similar to a videoconference presentation.) We discussed each presentation, providing feedback to each other and receiving good feedback from the tutors. The experience was immensely valuable for me and I refer to the course notes every time I get involved in a media interview or important videoconference. Here are the tips that I recorded for my own benefit in that course and after subsequent videoconferencing opportunities.

- Eye contact is really important. The audience at the other end has to feel that you are talking to them so you need to be looking at them. Generally this means looking at the camera. This is not easy for many presenters. If you can maintain eye contact with the camera and imagine that you are talking to real people then most of the rest falls into place.
- Sit upright (BBC; bum in back of chair).

- Do not clench your fists or do any of the many other displacement activities that you are fond of when you are nervous.
- Do not be shy.
- If the topic is not one that you know very well you will tend to pause (to think or to say 'um') too often. You need to rehearse aloud difficult explanations; not word for word, but just so that you are confident that you can explain it effectively.
- You will always run out of time.
- Do not put on a special voice. My children tell me that I have a special voice when I attempt to explain something and I find it difficult to get out of this 'lecturing mode'.
- Do use your hands to add effect but avoid rapid movements.
- Do not breath loudly or too close to the microphone.
- Do not be persuaded to give a presentation in this form that will take more than 8–10 minutes, unless you know that you are very good! If you have more to say than this then you need a more sophisticated videoconferencing set-up.

Key issue: feedback and evaluation

Not everyone has the opportunity to attend this sort of course but the issues are very real for everyone who will make use of videoconferencing. How you look and sound will influence how participants in the videoconference react to you. How you think that you look and sound will influence your own confidence in your ability to videoconference. So how do you look and sound in the videoconference environment? For most of us the answer is to borrow a camera, record some presentation activity and play it back.

I always advise people to record and playback with a supportive audience. If possible you need feedback from different perspectives. You might not be particularly happy with how you look and sound but colleagues can give a different perspective. You might think that you said 'um' too often, but your audience might not have noticed. Balanced feedback, good and bad, from a variety of sources will be helpful to you. Note that I said supportive audience. Generally you want people who will be honest but also people who understand the challenges because they are going through the same demanding circumstances themselves. Much of this is described in general terms in Chapter 5 but here we focus on feedback on your video presentation.

A tutor at Hillside studios gave me the following feedback characterized as an appraisal. (It was anonymous, not signed and it is about me so I guess that there are no particular copyright issues.)

Kerry always sounded enthusiastic and pleased to speak. His early interviews were responsive at times, with some brief answers, but he learned to take control and extend his answers to bring in his own agenda. Though his points were always made, however, they were not always totally clear or memorable. Specific examples will help.

On television, Kerry looks a little 'wild and woolly' – and without careful preparation, is in danger of appearing ill-focused. His final Down The Line interview was well controlled and persuasive. His eye-contact was good and his energy was better 'harnessed'. He backed up his arguments with examples and evidence, and extended his answers so well that the presenter was virtually redundant! Kerry has a committed 'chap-next-door' image – as one delegate described him, a 'house trained Bellamy'. He just needs to focus his enthusiasm, without losing his energy and charm.

It is important to take the feedback seriously – if you don't, then it will not benefit you. Some say that you have to 'own' the feedback. It is no good at all saying to yourself that the viewers 'had it in for me', or 'couldn't possibly see where I was coming from'. There are some exceptions, when some feedback is just too critical. It leaves you nowhere to go and it is doesn't help you improve. Most feedback, however, is helpful. It is constructive and it is probably the best source of information about your presentation that you are likely to get.

So lets look at the feedback from my helpful anonymous Hillside tutor. This is incredibly balanced and constructive.

- It doesn't shy away from identifying my real problems (wild and woolly; danger of being ill-focused).
- It balances this with some good points (Wow, I have charm! No one has ever said that about me before, and the appraiser suggests that I improved during the course).
- It suggests key things that I need to address (careful preparation, examples and evidence, continue to work on eye contact).

Since that course I have worked hard to keep eye contact with the camera, interviewer or audience; to prepare challenging material; to be less wild and woolly; and to keep track of time. My confidence has also developed with time and experience.

The real issue about feedback and evaluation relates to your confidence in how you look and sound to distant colleagues. If you are unsure how you will come across or if you are determined that you do not look or sound good then this is really bad for you. Lack of confidence will generally reduce your ability to present, no matter how good you actually look and sound to an impartial viewer. This issue is explored in other areas of this book, but we should develop it here in relation to the presence of the camera.

Cameras are rarely seen as benign by presenters. They have an influence. I suggest below a personal view and one that is verging on discriminatory, but I say it here in an attempt to help. This is in part a gender issue and, whether I like it or not, I can only really describe the issue from one side.

- Many men, in my limited experience, actually think that they look good, most of the time. Looking in the mirror is generally a positive, confidence building experience for them. They do not need immediate visual feedback from others around them to confirm that everything is all right. Why should the camera make a difference? I always look good.
- Many women, however, do not have this viewpoint. They are more likely, in my limited experience, to worry about how they come across to distant viewers. If this describes you, my advice is always to seek feedback and evaluation opportunities that will allow you to have more confidence in how you look and sound.

Key issue: practice

As with many other aspects of presentation there is no real substitute for experience. Videoconferencing does, however, have the big advantage that it is often fairly easy to organize a practice. You can practise on your own in front of a camera. You can practise with distant colleagues using simple computer-top cameras (webcams) and proprietary software such as NetMeeting.

Practice and experience have demonstrated to me that I (and many others) need to keep track of the following details:

- Controlling the mute button: it is embarrassing to discover that distant colleagues could hear your personal conversation to colleagues in the same room, when you thought that you had pressed the mute button.
- Sitting still: some hand movement is good but I do need to control this.
- Balancing thirst with the need to go to the toilet: most people get thirsty when they are nervous, so you need to have some water available otherwise your voice will dry up. But some videoconferences last long enough for participants to need a 'comfort break'. A good chairperson will insert reasonable breaks.

Web-casts, virtual learning environments and live lectures at a distance

If you are asked to present to a conference, at a distance, or to many groups or individuals, at a distance, then these technologies may be right for the occasion. This applies in particular if you need to talk for more than a few minutes, if you need good control over your presentation resources, if you need to interact with the audience and if you need to have some control over the interaction. Web-casts, virtual classrooms and live lectures at a distance are used in a wide range of educational, promotional and conference situations and we are really just beginning to learn what they have to offer. For this analysis the key features for the presenter are the availability of feedback from the audience and the ability to directly control the resources used. There are significant technical differences between the various systems that can enable these interactions to occur but many presenters will not need to delve too deeply into this aspect of the underlying technology. However, we need some examples to work with.

Most conventionally the presenter will sit in an office or studio in one location and present to an audience in another. The presenter will be able to see and hear the audience via a monitor and speakers. The presenter will also be able to control, for example, a PowerPoint presentation that the audience can see. The presenter can talk with the audience, not just at them, and if he or she is good enough, provoke verbal interaction via a microphone placed to pick up loud voices from the audience. Sometimes a roving microphone is provided so that interaction is possible with individuals in the audience, or individuals can come forward to a stationary microphone. Live lectures at a distance can be good. They are different from recorded lectures as they can be highly interactive. Speakers who get used to presenting in this way can find it just as rewarding as 'doing it for real'. For me the most important aspect of a presentation is often the interaction with the audience and this can still be good at a distance.

More recently, the connectivity of the Internet has been harnessed to enable web-casts to occur. Let's avoid the technicalities. The presenter sits in front of a camera and microphone and interacts with a distributed audience using a range of media. The focus for this interaction will be a web page that everyone has on his or her own computer screen. The audience will see the presenter, generally within a small window on the webpage, and hear the speaker though their computer's speaker. Often the audience and the speaker will also communicate via an online synchronous discussion forum. If someone in the distributed audience has a question they will type it in to their computer. Everyone involved in the conference will see it. The presenter may or may not choose to answer it during the presentation. It is more likely that the presenter will attempt to answer all of the questions after the presentation. The online discussion forum is just one form of communication medium possible within the web-cast. Indeed web-casts are just one form of a complex of interactive media.

Virtual learning environments are extensively used in higher education and allow a wide range of interactions to occur between a presenter and audience. Some systems have virtual classrooms with interactive whiteboards where the presenter can draw or write to illustrate a point, but some interactive whiteboards are more interactive than others. Some allow distant users to control the pen. With systems as diverse and complex as this, many applications make use of teams of helpers. The key issues for the presenter relate to the control of complex resources and management of complex interactions.

Key issue: controlling complex resources

The problem here is that the resources that you will use are generally specific to particular proprietary software. PowerPoint itself is an exception in that it is almost universal. Most presenters get to know how to use it in its basic form so it should not present a problem. How the presenter accesses it, however, may depend on the circumstances. Some videoconferences will use NetMeeting. This allows the host site to pass control of PowerPoint to the presenter at a distance. The technology rarely gives problems to those who practise. Someone at the host site has to click the *Share Programme* button and allow the distant presenter to take control of it. Other resources require more investment in skills acquisition. Some systems do have a whiteboard that is similar to a real whiteboard in that you can write or draw on it. Some allow much more. These require new software skills that you will have to learn and practise if you are to use them well.

Key issue: controlling complex interaction

I have recently been involved in synchronous online discussions with small groups of distant colleagues. Some of these used, or attempted to use, video-links as well as online synchronous discussion boards. These small online conferences or tutorials enabled me to think about the particular issues involved in controlling complex online interactions that make use of typed text. In real-life interactive discussions, the presenter can respond to questions one at a time, often with the help of a chairperson. Questions and answers occur at the speed of speech. Online, where interactions occur at the speed of typing and often without the benefit of body language, presenters and others need to adjust.

- Elements of a discussion can easily occur out of order. By the time someone has typed a long sentence, the discussion has moved on. The presenter has to be careful to control these interactions and to make it clear when the discussion is moving on. Providing periodic summaries is a good move.
- The depth of debate can sometimes be limited by the medium. Developing a complex spoken argument is difficult enough, but typing it is much more time consuming and challenging. Many interactions will be short and appear to be trivial. It is important to anticipate this and try hard to develop good arguments with few words.

Group-to-group videoconferences

Group-to-group videoconferences are becoming more widely used. Often more than two groups are involved and in that case there is normally an intermediate *bridge* or *reflector* site involved as well, to integrate the interactions that have to occur between the groups. Each group sits in a room in their own office, institution or company and watches other groups on their own monitor. Each group has its own videoconferencing equipment. Generally one member of each group has some control over the equipment. He or she can set the volumes of microphones and loudspeakers and if necessary set local microphones to mute (to enable a brief private within-group conversation to occur). Generally each group has some control over the camera used to relay its own image to the other groups. This set-up is often used in research and business environments to conduct meetings, discussions and small conferences at a distance. Perhaps individuals in one group will give a series of presentations to the other groups one day, and other groups respond on other occasions. Perhaps everyone gathers to hear what one individual has to say.

So, let's assume that there are four groups in four different rooms on the planet, using all sorts of fantastic technology to enable them to videoconference together. You have distributed some information to everyone in all groups by e-mail (perhaps with the agenda and papers for the meeting). Everyone has in front of them a transcript of your presentation or a set of PowerPoint slides. They know what's coming and they are waiting for you to explain yourself. If you haven't prepared and practised, the first thing that you will notice is that there is only one group displayed on the monitor in front of you, generally the last group that spoke or made a noise. You might not be sure who is displayed on the monitors of the other groups? Will they be looking at you? Will they be able to hear you? So you clear your throat and start to speak; quietly because you are a little nervous. Twenty seconds into your presentation you start to really worry. The group displayed in your monitor has not changed and they seem to be chatting to themselves. Your own group can hear you but you rapidly lose confidence that other groups can. You stop talking and feel very silly.

As described in the other scenarios, not feeling confident about what the audience is seeing and hearing is very disconcerting. It will put you off. What has happened? Generally these multi-group conferences work via a central system that receives sound and video input from all sites. Sound is then sent out to all groups but video signals are only sent from one. Which one? How does it decide which one? Generally the switching is voice-activated. The group making the most noise is the group whose images are relayed to all others. Just as with real discussions in unregulated environments, shy, quiet people do not stand a chance! That's why polite civilized society invented chairpeople (traditionally not the shy, quiet type) and why Parliament really does need a Speaker.

Group-to-group videoconferences generally use voice-activated image-switching (although some allow a chairperson to have control over this important function).

If you had known this you would have not been so concerned that other groups might not have been able to hear you. They probably could have. You were probably right to be concerned that you could still see the images of another group on your monitor. It might have indicated that your voice was too quiet to have switched the relayed video signal from another group to yours. But then different systems are configured in different ways and in an ideal configuration you should not be left looking at your own image. However, you were certainly right to be concerned that the other group seemed to be chatting!

In this group-to-group setting, the answers to two of the questions posed above – Will my normal presentation skills work in front of a camera? Will the technology place particular demands on me? – are probably No and Yes, respectively.

Key issue: how to be seen and heard in group-to-group videoconferences

As with other settings there is no real substitute for experience. Seek opportunities to practise in low-stakes conferences and meetings. Try to videoconference with others out of the formal conference environment altogether. You may find there are other participants from other sites equally worried about the conference. Contact them and try to arrange a private videoconference session. Practise with different settings on the camera and microphone. Set the microphone level to a reasonable setting, one that does cause the system to relay your image to the other groups. Then follow the guidance given below:

- Do not be shy. Sit up and speak up. If you are slightly timid in a real-life setting you will be mouse-like in this form of videoconference. You must have the microphone near to you. Much of the advice presented in the camera craft section applies to group-to-group videoconferences. If you want people at the other end to feel as if you are looking at them then you need to look at the camera.
- Even if you cannot see other groups it is extremely useful if you can use the technology to see the image that they see. Most videoconferencing systems have the capacity to show a small additional window in each monitor or they

have a separate monitor. This displays the image that is being sent out by your own camera. Use it! It is a great boost to your own confidence. (It is sometimes known as the confidence monitor.) So ask the IT technician to set it up this way, or find out how to do it yourself. Perhaps, at the same time, ask for a sound test to ensure that your voice is clearly transmitted.

- During the introduction to the conference check which image is shown on the monitor when you or a colleague in your group is talking and then when someone from another group is talking. Use this time to determine how long the delay is between someone else speaking and when the image relayed to the monitor changes. This delay will apply to your presentation too. You will need to say something to ensure that the audience sees you, before you start on the important bits!

- Seek real-time feedback. If you cannot see the other groups you will have to make the most of sounds. Yawns and the sound of doors closing are a bad sign. How long will you speak for? Perhaps you need to design into your presentation an opportunity for a brief discussion after a few minutes. In that way you will get some feedback and hopefully can proceed with confidence.

- Cope with coughs! If someone in one group has a loud and persistent cough then the voice activated switching might operate at inappropriate times. Not only will the cougher be heard by everyone but his or her image will be relayed to all groups as well. Isn't technology great? You will have to take control of the situation. When the cougher stops coughing perhaps you need to speak just a bit louder to switch the cameras back to you. A good chairperson will have asked other sites to mute their microphones.

Even with all of this in place there are many aspects of group-to-group videoconferences that can go wrong. Good group-to-group conferences do need good chairing. A shy or incompetent chairperson will not be able to take command of the proceedings. They will probably fail to invite speakers one at a time and prove unable to control a lively discussion. In a similar way, many group-to-group conferences need a good facilitator within each group. The facilitator's role will be to control the camera and control the mute button on the microphone. Generally they will be expected to book the facilities, prepare the room for the conference and be ready to troubleshoot when things go wrong. To some extent these issues do not relate directly to the technology but the technology certainly has an effect.

Other aspects of videoconferencing may also be out of your control but they are influenced by what you and others do. The quality of the sound and images in a videoconference is often limited by the bandwidth available in the connections. Highest quality is obtained when large images are transmitted at high frame rates. To make optimum use of limited bandwidth, signals are digitally compressed before transmission and the frame rate is adjusted according to the bandwidth available. A very important part of this protocol is that elements of images that do not change from frame to frame are not compressed and transmitted. Relatively simple images of stationary people can be transmitted at high quality. Rapidly changing images resulting from movement and bright, colourful, complex patterned clothing will be transmitted with poor quality. Therefore, wear bland clothing and when the camera is on you try to stay relatively still.

CASE STUDY 7.1
Presenting at a conference via a video-link

I had arranged to present a paper at the Annual Association for Learning Technologies Conference in Edinburgh, 2001. It was more than a simple research presentation; it was a panel discussion. In this format, three or four speakers present individually but on a common theme. The panel members do not have to agree with each other and indeed the discussion is often better if they do not. I had suggested the panel topic and invited five other speakers to join me. Three were partners in a multi-institutional research project that I was involved in and two were from a different research group that had different views on the topics being discussed. Within my own research group I had differing points of view from my partners. The discussion promised to be interesting. I travelled from Southampton to Edinburgh in good time for the conference but had to travel home on the first day of the conference, as my wife was rushed to hospital following an earlier accident. Two days later, on the day of the presentation, I was in Southampton, unable to contribute to the conference presentation that I had organized.

The conference presentation was about using video. We were all interested in using the power of video to support communication and learning. My colleagues were not going to let a few hundred miles prevent me making my contribution and my wife's health was improving. Colleagues in Edinburgh arranged for basic videoconferencing facilities (a connection to the Internet and a computer attached to a video projector and loud speaker) to be available in the presentation room. Colleagues in Southampton helped me to establish desktop videoconferencing on my computer. Additional communication was established by mobile phone. I sat at my desk, looked at the camera and spoke to prepared PowerPoint slides. The conference could see and hear me. I could hear the chairperson but I could not see anyone so I had to present with minimal feedback. (Partly as a result of this I did run over time.)

The presentation itself was OK for me; but not better than OK, at the time. As I was talking I had the sides in front of me and I think that I integrated the various aspects of the presentation reasonably. I do remember losing confidence on a couple of occasions. (Could they hear me? Were my examples relevant to that particular group? Was I going on for too long?). I realized that the presentation that I had planned to give in a face-to-face setting was not the best that I could do in this largely one-way videoconference setting. But I reasoned that the chairperson would comment if things went too off course. At the end some questions were relayed to me via the chairperson.

The presentation was generally well received. Feedback after the conference suggested that the participants particularly valued the use of the technology as part of the process of discussing the technology. For me, what started off as a nightmare developed into a positive experience. I would definitely seek opportunities to present via video-link again and not necessarily as a last resort. It built my confidence.

Some background information on videoconferencing technology

Making a start

Many people start off videoconferencing with friends using Microsoft's Windows NetMeeting. To get this running you will need to install NetMeeting from your Windows CD-ROM, buy and install a web-cam and microphone and check that your computer has a sound card. These, and related software and hardware items will come with instructions designed to help you (although you may not think so at the time). Persevere and adopt a trial and error approach. Eventually you will discover that if you, and your communication partner, have set up the system properly, then starting a videoconference is as simple as clicking on a call button.

To make a call you will need to know the call identity of your friend's computer. Most often we use IP (Internet Protocol) addresses. To find out your computer's IP address you need to start NetMeeting and click on 'Help' and 'About Windows NetMeeting' in the menu bar. The text box that appears will tell you your IP address. When you type this in you must keep the spaces, numbers and dots in the correct places!

Different forms of videoconferencing

When you videoconference using NetMeeting, simple web-cams and the Internet, you will probably be using the simplest networked or IP (Internet Protocol) form of videoconferencing. Depending on where you connect from you will either be accessing the Internet via a modem and telephone line or via a LAN (local area network). The quality of the images and sound will depend on the available bandwidth in the Internet and the connection to your computers. It is not always good enough!

Moving up in terms of complexity and cost, you may videoconference via the Internet using an ISDN Connection. ISDN (Integrated Services Digital Network) is the international standard for digitally-based telecommunications. ISDN can improve standard telephone lines by providing the same dial-up convenience, but with improved signal-carrying capacity. The basic ISDN standard provides one digital channel with a transfer rate of 64K per second. For example, ISDN2 provides two 64K channels, ISDN6 provides six, and so on.

There are other ways to link your computer to the Internet to provide videoconferencing. These include the use of Cable Modems, ADSLs (Asymmetric Digital Subscriber Lines) and low cost satellite feeds.

The highest quality videoconferencing is provided by direct ISDN connections, the main advantage of which is that audio and video transfers take place without having to compete for Internet bandwidth with other users and they are not liable to variations in Internet traffic.

Videoconferencing glossary

- *Bandwidth*   Some forms of communication contain little information or content (e.g. yes or no) but others, such as a moving image, contain a vast amount. The capacity of the communication channel to carry this information is loosely termed its bandwidth. The complexity of a transmitted message is often limited by the bandwidth available.
- *Bridge*   A bridge is an ISDN switching point that enables more than two sites to videoconference with each other. The bridge uses some form of switching to ensure that each site sees the site that is most important at the time. For example, UKERNA (The United Kingdom Education and Research Networking Association) provides a multipoint ISDN-based videoconference bridge (http://www.ja.net/). A reflector is an Internet site that allows multi-way videoconferencing for videoconferences using the Internet rather than direct ISDN lines.
- *Codec*   A codec is the software used by communication devices to encode and decode audio and video information.
- *Compression*   Complex signals are rarely carried complete. They are normally compressed so that the information carried is as small as possible to maximize the use of available bandwidth. Most video compression systems eliminate elements of the picture that do not change between frames.
- *Frame rate*   Moving pictures are generally made up from a number of still pictures or frames. A low frame rate gives a jerky video image but can be sent over communication channels with limited bandwidth. The minimum acceptable frame rate will depend on your aspirations for quality and

the amount of movement in the image. If you need to see lips move or sign language you will need a high frame rate and sufficient bandwidth to carry it.

How effective is videoconferencing?

Videoconferencing has found many applications in the business and education world. There are many economic stimuli to its continuing development because it is seen by many to serve a purpose. In some settings it appears that it is so important to see who you are talking to, that users will endure any number of technical problems and be happy to tolerate poor quality interactions. For others the quality and reliability of the interaction is far more important and many choose not to use this technology for these reasons. Research and development is therefore on two broad fronts; development of the technology itself and development and evaluation of the processes of videoconferences. Largely due to the stimulus of distance learning and eLearning, a particularly significant body of evaluative information is now available on the use of videoconferencing in education (BECTA, 2003). Some other key reports are referenced in the bibliography of this book. These documents provide links to a body of case studies and analyses to answer the question of how effective videoconferencing can be. Most of these will attempt to place the question in the context of the precise circumstances of the conference. Many will insist that we ask the question in relation to precisely configured intended outcomes. Despite all of this I still meet academic staff who tell me that videoconferencing 'does not work'; and that the experience for the audience is never the same as 'having the person there in real life'. Against that I read sound academic evaluations of where videoconferences have been effective in educational settings (for example Carville and Mitchell 2000, on the operation of a distance-learning course using videoconferencing).

One aspect, that I hope will receive more evaluative research in the future, relates to the potential of videoconferences to produce frank discussions. I have often felt that meetings held by videoconference can get to the heart of an issue more quickly than face-to-face meetings. People are less polite and deferential at a distance. Perhaps they feel safer. Research is beginning to find evidence for this. Sharpe and her colleagues in Singapore found that real-time conferencing tends to promote more frank discussion and equal opportunity among participants on teacher-training programmes (Sharpe et al., 2000). If this is the effect that you are seeking then videoconferencing may be effective for you.

Summary

Videoconferencing must be experienced to be believed. It also has to be experienced in circumstances when the technology and people are well prepared and well organized. As with all activities that involve technology, there is a lot of work involved and things can go wrong. The benefits must outweigh the disadvantages. This chapter is all about maximizing these benefits.

I am an enthusiast for videoconferencing. I do like travelling and I will travel almost anywhere for some good fishing. But sitting in the train, or on a motorway, for several hours to get to a meeting that might only last one or two hours is rarely fun. We will all have our own cost–benefit analysis in particular circumstances, but the more often videoconferencing works for me, the better the face-to-face meeting has to be to ignore its possibilities!

References

BECTA (British Educational Communications and Technology Agency) (2003) 'What the research says about videoconferencing in teaching and learning', http://www.becta.org.uk/page documents/research/wtrs_vidconf.pdf (accessed 26 November 2003).

Carville, S. and Mitchell, D.R. (2000) 'It's a bit like star trek: the effectiveness of videoconferencing', *Innovations in Education and Training International,* 37 (1): 42–9.

Hillside Training (2003) http://www.hillside-studios.co.uk/training.htm (accessed 19 November 2003).

Sharpe, L., Chun, Hu, Crawford, L., Gopinathan, S., Ngoh Moo, S. and Wong, A.F.L. (2000) 'Multipoint desktop videoconferencing as a collaborative learning tool for teacher preparation', *Educational Technology*, 40 (5): 61–3.

UKERNA (2003) 'UKERNA video conference meetings: how to get the best out of a video conference meeting', http://www.video.ja.net/usrg/U_page4.html (accessed 17 November 2003).

A videoconferencing checklist for new presenters

This checklist is specifically for videoconferencing. It is designed to be used in conjunction with the more generic checklist at the end of Chapter 8. In preparing for your videoconference presentation, have you attended to the following tasks yet?

- Practised what you want to say in a conventional setting.
- Practised informally with a friend or colleague, using NetMeeting for example.
- Received feedback on your presentation skills as seen via the camera.
- Practised eye contact with the camera.
- Practised informally using the same equipment as will be used for real.
- Discussed your role with technical staff locally and at the distant venue.
- Discussed your role with the person who will chair the presentation.
- Done what is necessary to feel confident about your own appearance.
- Chosen clothes without zigzags or fine patterns.

8

Delivering the Successful Presentation and What to Do When Things Go Wrong

Key concepts in this chapter:

■ How presenters know when things are not working out and what to do about it.

■ To accurately time your presentation while you are giving it, you really need to know when you started.

■ Ensure that you speak with confidence and enthusiasm.

■ Technology does not always fail but sometimes it does. Be prepared.

■ Do not expand your explanations beyond your preparations.

■ Is your subject as interesting to the audience as it is to you?

■ Disbelief is an easy non-verbal signal to pick up.

■ Inability to interact with the audience is the most frequent cause of a poor presentation.

■ Present at a level and pace to suit the audience; not to suit you.

■ Prepare your question and answer session with the same attention to detail as the rest of your presentation.

This chapter is primarily about delivering a successful presentation but it is also about what you should do when things start to go wrong. The aspects of presentations most likely to go awry were described in Chapter 1 and will be addressed again here in the form of potential solutions to problems. Naturally most of the solutions do rely on advanced planning along the lines of 'hope for the best but plan for the worst'.

But before we get that far we need to consider how presenters know when things are not working out. Members of the audience will not generally jump up and shout, 'rubbish'; nor will they throw things at you (although this might sometimes be kinder than what they actually do!). What can presenters do to ensure that they pick up the necessary signals? This basically comes down to your ability as a presenter to decentre, the concept developed in Chapter 2. If you always consider the position, experience and needs of the audience, even while you present to them, then you should be able to detect it when they are having problems with what you are saying and how you are saying it. Even with no verbal communication, you will be aware of their interest, needs and frustrations. It may be something dramatic, such as, they all stop writing at once, get up and leave. Perhaps more likely, one person leaves, paving the way for others. More subtle messages include flat, bored expressions; nose picking and nail cleaning; looking out of the window; secretive texting on mobile phones; or yawns. You do need to be tuned in to receiving and interpreting non-verbal communication. Will you detect a certain look in their eyes? Only if you look at their eyes!

Your potential problem areas

Late for the presentation

Not this time! See Chapter 6 for some ideas on avoiding this disaster.

(So your time has arrived! The person chairing your session is introducing you and you make your way to the front of the room.)

Timing

Many presentations are lost at this stage. For many of us, our carefully planned presentation depends on timing. To time your presentation accurately while you are giving it, you need to know when you started. So as you approach the front of the room, you should glance at the clock or at your watch and make a mental note of the time. If you have a stopwatch in your pocket, you need to start it now. You will have prearranged with the chairperson for a 5-minute warning toward, the end of your presentation; but when this comes you do not want to be surprised!

(You arrive confidently at the presentation desk and place your notes where you intended to. You move the papers that someone else left to somewhere where they will not be in your way. You make a mental note of the location of the lighting switches, computer, pointer, OHP, flip chart (clean page), whiteboard (clean, with pens and board rubber). You raise your head to look, with confidence, at everyone in the audience.)

Nerves

This is when nerves will fail if they are going to! Many successful presenters stumble over their first few words. Some manage to memorize the first lines of their presentation but many have discovered that they forget the most practised phrases when confronted by this particular moment. They resort to off-the-cuff comments and say something unintelligible or inappropriate or both. A sympathetic audience lets them off but you shouldn't rely on this. Those who forget, when they are nervous, need to have something written down ... just a few key words ... Thank Chairperson ... Thank organiser ... Thank audience ... Today I am going to spend 20 minutes ... Those who use presentation aids for their own benefit will have designed their presentation so that the first slide is something interesting for the audience and for them; something that they can engage with, with confidence and enthusiasm; and something that doesn't need the lights to be dimmed.

What if, after all that preparation, your mind really does 'go blank'. You have two alternatives. You can resort to using your written notes and perhaps you will only need to read a few lines before your 'brain re-engages' and you can move on. Another approach is to seek a diversion, which may just be to pour a drink of water and to sip it. As this should be a fairly automatic action it will give you the time to think about where you are in the presentation and what comes next. If you encounter problems later on in your presentation, it may help to recap your last major point; either repeat it or, if you are using visual aids, skip back to the previous slide. In my experience, audiences are very forgiving of this problem and will understand, and support, your attempts to overcome it. In this respect the audience is on your side, in particular because this might easily happen to them.

(You thank the chairperson and the organizers for inviting you. You say your prepared introduction and rapidly move into something really interesting that engages the audience from the start, and you speak with confidence and enthusiasm. In particular you remember all the advice about eye contact with the audience and you make fleeting contact with just about everyone in the room.)

Technology

What goes around comes around. Did you really think that the technology wouldn't fail when you were in the spotlight? Well, that was a surprise then! Technology does not always fail but sometimes it does. You need to be prepared in two ways. You need to have a back-up as described in Chapters 3 and 5. Perhaps some OHP transparencies or some printed notes. You also need a prepared plan to enable you to decide when to implement your back-up. How long will you wait for that elusive IT technician? How long to reboot that computer and how long to search for your program? If the data projector switched itself off, how long will you wait for its bulb to cool before it will start again?

Some people are blessed with great patience and are foolish enough to think that their audience is too. However, I am not patient, so if the technology fails me in a presentation, no matter whose fault it is, I move on to low-tech solutions. It is important to plan for this event. Perhaps, in a 20-minute presentation, you will plan to be patient for 2 minutes. My advice is to stick to your plan. Even if the IT technician promises that all will be fine in 1 more minute. Do not believe him. Move on. It is a little like the advanced planning needed before you bid at an auction. Decide what you can afford and do not be tempted to bid higher, no matter how tempting the moment is. Move on.

(You are prepared for all sorts of problems with the technology but the computer works well for you, this time.)

Lack of content

There are times when you discover that you really do not know your subject as well as you thought. As you try to explain things to the audience you realize that there are flaws in your arguments and that key detail is missing. Try as you might you cannot help bringing this to the audience's attention. You have an inner urge to abandon your prepared presentation and open your heart to the audience. You start to expand your explanations beyond your preparations. So now, not only do you think that your presentation is a sham, but your audience does as well. This is a vicious cycle that rapidly undermines your confidence in your ability to present.

After the presentation it generally looks different. If you were properly prepared you probably did know enough about your subject after all. You knew enough to know where knowledge turned to conjecture. This is, of course, a problem for all 'experts'. You know as much as there is to know about something and as you describe it to others you understand it better yourself. You see the limitations in current theory or the flaws in established paradigms. This is all part of learning but it is better to have learned to this level before the presentation rather than during it! Perhaps you did not rehearse enough.

There is, potentially, another factor here. It is always difficult to judge how much time it will take you to present your work. Even after repeated rehearsals, you know that it is possible to finish early or late. In 25 years of presenting, however, I have never run out of material to talk about. I very rarely finish early. I always have to make a real effort to finish on time. Nevertheless, I always include in my preparation more material than I need; just in case.

(Ten minutes into your presentation you see that you have spent too long on the introductory slides. At this rate, you will finish late. You make a note to speed up a bit over the middle section of your talk. You had intended to provide two examples to cover the next point; one will do.)

Boring content

Here you discover that your subject is not as interesting to the audience as it is to you. They haven't left yet but they look bored and they are fidgeting. Perhaps you are also bored and the audience is picking this up from your tone of voice or from your body language. Is your voice becoming a monotone? Is your face expressionless? Are your hands in your pockets?

It is your job to make the content of your presentation as interesting as it can be to the audience. It might not be inherently interesting but there must be some reason why you said that you would talk about it and why the audience turned up. You need to build on this and add some of your own enthusiasm to the occasion.

(You have spotted some early signs that some in the audience are not engaged. You decide that you need to use your second example rather than your first, to illustrate the next key point. The second example is more relevant to the audience in front of you. It will engage them better and it is a little more demanding to understand. You also make a conscious effort to look at people, even those folk at the back. You move around a bit more and make sure that your voice is adding emphasis at key moments.)

Is it believable?

Disbelief is an easy non-verbal signal to pick up. It is a real danger sign in any presentation. Either you are being dishonest or the audience is incorrectly interpreting your presentation in this way. Perhaps you said something that hadn't occurred to you as being inconsistent but did occur to the audience in this way. Perhaps you missed out a stage in your explanation. Perhaps your explanation is too complex for the audience. Once they start to doubt you, they are difficult to engage again.

How do professional salespeople cope? Not perhaps the professional selling a good product at a fair price, but the unprofessional selling a substandard product. They know that it is rubbish. Sometimes they know that you know that it is rubbish! Their key strength is that they give the impression that they trust the product that they are selling.

Whether by body language or by words, you need to ensure that you give the impression that you are an honest presenter. If there are obvious flaws in your argument you need to identify them. If there are hidden flaws then you need to acknowledge their existence. Honesty is always the best policy, but you have to prepare to be honest. In particular you need to have made an effort to look at your data from the perspective of the audience. Practising with feedback is an important element of this process, as described in Chapter 5.

(You had anticipated that some in the audience would doubt the results shown in your third graph. The results were not consistent with what others had demonstrated previously. You made a great effort to identify the differences and attempted to explain them. You also said that you would be happy to answer questions on this part of your work, either at the end of your presentation, or later in the day at the Poster Session. This went down well with the audience.)

Inability to interact with the audience

In my experience this is the most frequent cause of a poor presentation. Presenters bury their heads in a script and never look at the audience. Presenters become engrossed in their own work; they drop their head or stare at their own presentation visuals; they wander up and down with their hands in their pockets. They are self contained. People in the audience have no role in this presentation. They are not part of it. They do not feel involved so they switch off and read their programme asking themselves what comes next. They might as well not be here. You are wasting their time.

It doesn't have to be like that. You are there to help them understand your viewpoint on something important to you. Because of this, it is also important to you that you support the development of the audience's understanding. If you went too fast over an element of your argument and lost some of the audience, you want to know it, so that you can backtrack and cover the point better. For this to be possible you need to interact with the audience. Eye contact, relevant examples, hand movements and questioning all help. Key methods for interaction are described in Chapters 4 and 5.

(You have prepared for interaction. You are maintaining good eye contact with everyone in the audience. You do need to move around the table to ensure that you look at people in the far corner on occasions. Now you know this audience a little better you are able to choose your examples to suit them. You have also planned to ask a key question after Graph 5 and you have already decided which member of the audience will give you the answer. And, yes, you will remember to relay this answer back to the audience.)

You lose the audience

Level and pace should suit the audience, not you. If your presentation is too easy for the audience, or delivered too slowly, then they will get bored. If it is too difficult for them, or delivered too fast, they will also get bored, but in a different way. I have been to presentations where most of the audience clearly could not keep up with the presenter. Sometimes these were talks where the presenter made no attempt at all to discover how the audience was coping. Sometimes, particularly where the difficult bits were mathematical, it was clear that the presenter knew that the audience would not keep up but felt that it was his professional responsibility to present this way. The audience would just have to take his word that this is how it works and that it was necessary to see it in this detail. I strongly suspect that on some occasions the situation was designed to be like this; it gave the presenter a buzz of some sort to think that he was cleverer than the audience. Whether the main diagnosis is arrogance or the observance of a strange professional tradition, is not the point here. By any measure these are examples of poor presentation.

Let's assume that you will attempt to communicate with the audience and not just talk at them. You will want to spot the signs of frustration or boredom that indicate that the audience has missed something that you think is important. Then you will want to do something about it. Backtrack until you see signs of understanding.

The other significant cause of losing an audience is that you have adopted a structure that the audience did not follow. Perhaps you gave them no idea about how your presentation would develop. Perhaps you chose a structure that was too complex or too odd for that particular audience. Again, you will want to spot the signs of frustration and make some necessary corrections. Perhaps you just need to make it slightly more obvious where that last bit of information fitted in.

(You have nearly finished. You are as sure as you can be that they did keep up. Even the odd data in Table 1 produced the desired effect when you pointed it out. If they hadn't understood, they would not have responded in that way. Then when you asked for a show of hands about the predicament in Figure 3 you got an excellent response.)

Questions and answers

Most presentations have question and answer sessions at the end. So they should. But these need to be prepared with the same attention to detail as the rest of your presentation. You need to design your presentation to stimulate suitable questions and you need to be prepared to answer them. If unexpected questions arise this is to be celebrated, not feared. But your answers do need to be honest. If you do not know the answer, you need to say so.

One aspect of this stage of your presentation is important but always difficult to plan for. You have to 'think on your feet'. It is important that your question time does not drag on and on and slowly die a death, as your chairperson tries in vain to squeeze one last question out of a reluctant audience. If this happens, you will feel bad, even if it is not your fault. Be assertive. Be in control and make distinct finishing noises when you want to finish. As a last resort, if your chairperson doesn't finish the session when you want him to, finish it yourself, for example: 'I see that there are no more questions. I'll finish there and make way for the next speaker. Thank you.'

(You reach the end of your presentation, thank the audience for listening and invite questions. You have planned for this by introducing several themes in your presentation that were designed to stimulate interest without providing all of the answers. If they wanted to know more then they had to ask. Two of your anticipated questions were asked and a third was unexpected but not unwelcome. It provided an excellent final point for your presentation and enabled the chairperson to thank you and finish the session.)

A checklist

Checklists are difficult. For something as varied as presenting at conferences and meetings it will be impossible to be comprehensive, and some included items will not be relevant to some settings. In addition, some elements are complex and it does them no justice to condense them into a short phrase. But I think that some form of checklist should be useful to some readers. So in preparing for your presentation, have you attended to the following tasks yet?

Responded with enthusiasm to the invitation and asked for information about the audience, the nature and duration of your presentation, about the venue, the room and about its access to technology.	
Researched the audience and what they expect you do to.	
Reflected on your own abilities and on how these will influence your presentation.	
Planned the content and how you want to present it.	
Planned the structure of your presentation.	
Planned for interaction using questions, answers, eye contact and relevant examples.	

Planned how you will present yourself including what you will wear.	
Reflected on how presentation aids could help.	
Designed and developed your presentation aids.	
Prepared back-ups of your presentation aids.	
Ensured that the start of your presentation will engage the audience and help you overcome initial nerves.	
Rehearsed your presentation yourself until you are happy with it.	
Practised your presentation in front of colleagues and asked them for constructive feedback.	
Rehearsed it again after implementing aspects of the feedback.	
For a high-stakes presentation, rehearsed it again using your back-up presentation aids.	
Checked that the person organizing the conference, seminar or meeting is happy with your title and, if possible, abstract. Ensured that you have given them, or the person who will chair your presentation, enough details about you for them to introduce you.	
Double checked the venue, date and time and then made travel plans.	
Discussed technology with the venue's technical support team. Can you send them your presentation aids by e-mail? Will they test them in situ?	
Travelled to the venue and arrived in good time.	
Gained access to the room to load and check your presentation aids, investigate lighting, pointer, obstacles and computer controls including mouse. Checked equipment needed as a back-up.	
Ensured that you have a watch or that there is a clock available, and that you check it when you start so that you know when to finish.	
Reflected on your back-up plans and on what will induce you to switch to them.	
Gone to the loo (lavatory, toilet) and returned in good time. Poured some water into a glass and sipped it.	
You are now ready to enjoy the occasion but keep an eye on your audience!	

Summary

This chapter accompanies your successful presentation, where you have adequately designed it, prepared yourself and organized the venue. Because you paid all this attention to detail, just about everything went well. But the chapter has also been with you when things started to go off course, encouraged you to be aware of problems just about to occur and helped you to take preventative measures. If you read this chapter first, primarily because you had limited time to plan for this presentation, then I do hope that you will now delve into the rest of the book. I wrote Chapter 9 for readers planning, in the longer term, for a future that involves presenting at conferences, seminars and meetings.

9

How to Get Better

Key concepts in this chapter:

▌ Diagnosing your problems is difficult but essential.

▌ How staff development workshops can help.

▌ Feedback can be really helpful to you.

▌ Evaluation is tough but really useful.

▌ Books, and other learning resources, may help you with specific changes.

▌ Overcoming *ums* and *ers* may need long-term endeavour; you know?

▌ Practice makes perfect.

▌ Anything that boosts your confidence will probably help you present.

We considered whether or not, and how, our presentations could improve in Chapters 1 and 2. Having decided that they could, we then set about designing in Chapter 4 after exploring the potential contribution of presentation aids in Chapter 3. Having prepared ourselves, and the venue, in Chapters 5, 6 and 7, things still went wrong, so in Chapter 8, we did some last minute first-aid. We have now come full circle and we need to think seriously about how to do this thing before we attempt it again. What can we do in the long term to improve our ability to present?

Naturally the answer to this depends, to an extent, on what precisely is wrong with how we have done it so far. Feedback and experience have taught *me* that I tend to wander off topic and not finish on time. I also physically move around too much. My spelling deteriorates when I am stressed. I have a tendency to rely just a little too much on my presentation aids. Nothing too drastic.

Can I improve? Should I try to improve? Over the years I have developed strategies that allow me to cope with all of these problems and I do probably cope to the extent that most audiences would not notice that these are problems. I use my presentation aids, just a bit, to keep me on track so that I do not wander off topic. I practise to get my timing right and I try hard to check the time before I start so that I know when to finish. Yes, I move around and I do use my hands a lot; but I am sure that this channels my nervous energy away where it does least harm. It also helps me interact with the audience. I have a range of well-developed strategies that enable me to avoid having to spell difficult (for me) words in front of a large audience. Even so, I am not entirely happy that I have reached the peak of my presentation abilities, yet. Currently I am focusing my 'improvement energy' into experimenting with a wider range of presentation aids (including video) and finding the confidence to speak without any presentation aids at all.

Ah! It slipped out. Did you notice? *Finding the confidence.* So much of self-improvement seems to relate to confidence. I know that I can stand in front of an audience and speak intelligently for considerable periods of time. I taught biology in higher education for more than 20 years. Yet in a presentation setting the stakes just seem higher. I guess that being able to do something – and being confident that I can do it, under pressure, in front of an audience, are two different things. So perhaps there are two stages to long-term improvement. I need to tackle my specific problems and then I need to address my more general levels of confidence.

But that is enough about me. What was your problem? In the list below I indicate chapters in this book that I hope will help you address your particular problems; but all elements then lead into the more generic content later in this chapter.

- Was it a lack of interaction? This is most commonly associated with poor body language, particularly lack of eye contact with people in the audience. Did you lose the audience? Perhaps you looked up from your notes to see bored or blank faces? Perhaps you asked a question that no one answered? Perhaps no one asked you a question? Re-read Chapters 4 and 5.
- Was it poor timing? Do you tend to run over time or have long pauses in your presentation? Re-read Chapter 4.
- Did you struggle with the technology? Did it all go wrong, yet again? Re-read Chapter 3.

- Were you excessively nervous? Did you shake and forget what you wanted to say? Re-read Chapter 5 and focus on boosting your confidence.
- Did you struggle to communicate effectively with the audience? Did what you had to say sound boring; even to you? Were you trying to deceive the audience, perhaps even deceive yourself? Re-read Chapter 4, but Chapter 1 also has some important content on these topics.

Having re-read the rest of this book and practised everything in it, you are probably ready to embark on your long-term quest for presentation excellence! Each of the subsequent sections provides information on a particular approach but I think that it is important to stress that building your own confidence in your ability to present is as important as building skills.

Workshops and how they work

I have run 'continuing professional development' workshops on presenting at conferences for several years, in higher education and in related settings. Presenting at conferences is such an important feature of academic life that most universities run workshops on this topic. Most workshops in most settings will address most of the material in this book. Small groups of participants will discuss attributes of presentations that they like, get to know each other, then give short presentations (often recorded on video camera) and then provide balanced feedback to each other.

These workshops, in my experience, serve three important functions:

- Obviously they are designed to allow presenters to benefit from feedback from peers. If a participant has a particular problem, the workshop should at least discover it.
- Less obviously, but often more importantly, the workshop should open the way for participants to elicit and benefit from further feedback. Some participants are naturally cautious about feedback; often they have benefited, in the past, only from negative feedback. The workshop environment provides an opportunity for participants to benefit from balanced constructive feedback from peers who are in the same circumstances and who have no

particular grudge. Participants should feel more confident about asking for feedback in the future.

- The third function of the workshop is to boost the participants' confidence. They should leave with these thoughts on their minds: 'Hmmn, my presentation was not bad. I did get lots of positive feedback. OK, there are a couple of problems but I know how I am going to tackle them. I am glad I came to this workshop and I am sure that my next presentation will be much better than the last one was.'

(Workshop facilitators: if most of your participants do not leave your workshop in this frame of mind then your workshop is not working! How will you know? It should be evaluated to demonstrate how successfully these outcomes have been achieved!).

The role of feedback and evaluation

The importance of feedback has been stressed in several sections of this book. How to give it, how to receive it and act on it, and how to ask for it, are all important aspects of your continuing endeavour to improve your presentation skills. The feedback may confirm what you already know about yourself or it may just provide a stimulus for your continued reflection on how you present. This is all useful. As described above, workshops are particularly good for putting you in a position where feedback is given willingly and in a helpful spirit.

Actually this feedback is just one contribution to an overall *evaluation* of your presentation. You want to know how successful each of your presentations have been so you need to evaluate them against a set of predetermined desired outcomes. The world of higher education is currently obsessed with evaluation and rightly so. In fact, more evaluation would help us discover more about learning and teaching; and about particular styles of presentation.

Educational researchers know a lot about evaluation and a wide range of strategies have evolved to cope with teaching situations every bit as demanding and difficult as your presentation. Yet the average presenter would not consider using a formal evaluation approach. Certainly the average presenter would run a mile from any notion of external evaluation. That leaves us with self-evaluation.

This is unlikely to be as robust as evaluation by an independent evaluator, but is nonetheless a successful and respected educational tool.

The basic notion of educational evaluation draws extensively from research methodologies, commonly used in the social sciences, known as action-research. Action-research contrasts with experimental research in that it includes and accepts the researcher as part of the process and does not try to control the process by keeping some variables constant. In the challenging circumstances typical of education it is almost impossible to control anything! The concept has been extrapolated to evaluation, rather than more formal research, by several authors including Rothman and Friedman who promote what they call Action Evaluation (Friedman and Rothman, 2002). The process goes something like this: a presenter draws up a set of objectives for her next presentation that will test out some change in style or content; she then designs and implements an evaluation strategy; gives the presentation; evaluates it against the desired outcomes; decides how effective the change was; then alters the change in an attempt to improve its effect even more.

There are many styles of evaluation. I like the approach recommended by Stake (1967). Information in the form of descriptive or quantitative data is divided into 'antecedents' (what happened before the event), 'transactions' (what happened during the event) and 'outcomes' (what the event's results were). For each, a separate description of 'intentions' (what you hoped would happen) and 'observations' (what actually happened) is made and congruence between them ascertained. For presentations, the data could take many forms. You could ask a supportive friend to sit in and record aspects of your presentation (an approach not too dissimilar to the basis of peer review of teaching). You could design a practice-presentation where you ask members of the audience to complete an 'evaluation checklist' (probably more formally an 'audience perception survey'). You could arrange to have your presentation recorded on videotape and 'score it yourself' using an evaluation checklist. However you collect data, an important stage is how you interpret and act on this data. Like learning, this involves you reflecting on what you have done.

A number of evaluation checklists are available to help you. As described in Chapter 2, many educational institutions regard the ability to present as an important academic or key skill. As such they support the acquisition of presentation skills and assess student performance. Assessment nowadays needs to be set against predetermined outcomes, often with defined assessment criteria to determine the level of performance. (Just imagine if this occurred at your next conference with you at the receiving end!) Whatever the rights and wrongs of the process the resulting assessment grids could provide a useful, if non-theoretical, evaluation checklist for you. There are probably dozens of these checklists available 'on the web'. I typed in 'presentation skills' as a search term in Google and found several. Two are listed in this book's bibliography (but they may not still be there when you look!)

You can use the theoretical relationship between spoken-language performance-indicators and higher mental-process competencies proposed by Dance (Dance and Zac-Dance, 1996). This has the advantage of linking each performance indicator with a theoretical competency. Using this relationship you can at least hope, that by tackling the performance indicator, you will be improving its underlying mental competency. That's the theory.

Alternatively you can use the categories of presentation attributes developed in this book: content, structure, interaction, self-presentation and use of presentation aids. Five categories of feedback may well be enough to work with. If you want to add more detail, why not use the list of 'what makes a good presentation' given in Chapter 1 (for example, in Table 1.1). Even better, design your own checklist based on Chapter 1, incorporating your own 'six things that you thought were good about the presentation' that you recorded in Chapter 1's brainstorming exercise.

Whatever approach you choose to collecting data please remember that the data on its own is not enough. You need to interpret this data in relation to what you intended would happen before, during and after your presentation.

Do books have a role?

I think that books have a role here. It is always fun finding out for yourself how to do something but generally more productive making personal developments that relate to what others have done. A book can enable you to relate your experiences to the experiences of others and to a theoretical framework; should one exist. A good book may be a poor second to a good workshop but at least it is there to refer to when you want it. The general bibliography at the end of this book provides references to a number of (other) books that may be helpful.

Longer-term problems

It might be that attending a workshop, receiving feedback or your own self-evaluation has identified or emphasized a problem that seriously influences your ability to present. In my own experience I have come across presenters who discover that they have a problem only after seeing themselves on a video replay. The most common of these is the presenter who says, 'um', 'er' or 'you know' before or after every phrase. I suspect that there are many reasons for these problems and we all do this to a certain extent. Some of these problems become more severe when we are nervous and that is why they emerge so strongly in presentation situations. Sometimes I am surprised that presenters with these problems have not had better feedback from friends in more informal circumstances. But often it is a case of friends not wanting to tell you that you have a problem. Even in workshops, other participants often feel embarrassed about pointing out these particular problems. When the presenter is confronted by a video recording with one or two 'ums' or 'ers' in every sentence, then they cannot escape it. Solving the problem is more difficult and is almost certainly a long-term endeavour. Self-diagnosis is probably not a good idea. Speech therapists separate language disorders from speech disorders. Each is diagnosed and treated differently. Some speech patterns are described as agrammatic; particularly those that use excessive redundant stereotyped phrases.

I know of presenters who have overcome these problems without resorting to speech therapy, but if the problem is serious and getting in the way, then speech therapy may be the way to go.

There is no substitute for experience

Neither books nor workshops can help you unless you gain experience. I always advise people to put themselves out to gain experience at presenting their work. Find opportunities and make use of them for your own personal development. In some respects this is because, many years ago, I was advised to do this and I know that it benefited me, both career-wise and in terms of my own confidence in my ability to present. Following a period of postdoctoral research in New Zealand, I was returning to the UK to take up a lectureship. I had intended to travel straight home but I was persuaded to make use of the opportunity to visit universities on the way. Each visit entailed at least one research presentation. In a matter of three weeks I visited and presented at universities in British Columbia, Washington State, Oregon and California. The presentations, and my skills, changed considerably in this period. After each presentation I was able to reflect on what went right and what went wrong and make changes; changes that I could implement and test just a few days later. It was a good experience for me.

Boost your confidence

This really is the 'last resort' section of this book! In my experience, confidence is such an important factor in successful presentation that perhaps *almost* anything that boosts your confidence in your ability to present will help you. For me, the specific sequence of activities that I undertake before each presentation, described in Chapter 5, is enough for my 'high stakes' presentations. Then the processes described in this chapter involving the action-research cycle of evaluation are sufficient to maintain my general confidence. My next presentation will be good; quite possibly better than my last one.

But this may not be enough for everyone. Some people turn to therapists, some to personal spiritual advisers. There are many programmes available to enhance a participant's assertiveness. All of these, and others, might result in a boost to a presenter's confidence. Outside of education it is not unusual to find large public relations firms involved. Politicians, in particular, receive extensive training to sound, and look, good at the next party conference. Sometimes it works. But sometimes it doesn't. Perhaps it is possible to boost a presenter's confidence further than their skills!

Final words

Good luck with your next presentation and remember to hope for the best, but plan for the worst. If you meet me at a conference somewhere, please do not expect me to deliver a perfect presentation. Presenting is tough enough as it is, without having to live up to that expectation!

333

References

Dance, F.E.X. and Zac-Dance, C.C. (1996) *Speaking your Mind: Private Thinking and Public Speaking*, 2nd edn. Dubuque, IA: Kendall/Hunt.

Friedman, V.J. and Rothman, V. (2002) 'Action evaluation for knowledge creation in social-education programs', Online at http://www.aepro.org/inprint/papers/knowledge.html (accessed 3 March 2004).

Stake, R.E. (1967) 'The countenance of educational evaluation', *Teachers College Record* 68 (7): 523–40.

Brief Bibliography

On preparing your presentation aids

Orchard, D.M., Perow, B.D., Frakes, K. and Reed, T. (2000) *Figuratively Speaking in the Computer Age: Techniques for Preparing and Presenting Presentations.* Tulsa: AAPG.

Tufte, E.R. (1983) *The Visual Display of Quantitative Information.* Cheshire, CT: Graphics Press.

Tufte, E.R. (1997) *Visual Explanations: Images and Quantities, Evidence and Narrative,* Cheshire, CT: Graphics Press.

On non-verbal communication

Argyle, M. (1974) *The Psychology of Interpersonal Behaviour,* 2nd edn. Harmondsworth, UK: Penguin.

Argyle, M. (1988) *Bodily Communication,* 2nd edn. New York: Methuen.

Mehrabian, A. (1981) *Silent Messages: Implicit Communication of Emotions and Attitudes.* Belmont, CA: Wadsworth.

Wainwright, G.R. (1985) *Body Language.* Sevenoaks, UK: Hodder and Stoughton.

On more conventional lecturing

Brown, G. (1978) *Lecturing and Explaining.* London: Methuen.

Brown, S. and Race, P. (2002) *Lecturing.* London: RoutledgeFalmer.

Gibbs, G., Habershaw, S. and Habershaw, T. (1984) *53 Interesting Things to Do in Your Lectures.* Bristol: Technical and Educational Services.

Habershaw, S., Gibbs, G. and Habershaw, T. (1992) *53 Problems with Large Classes.* Bristol: Technical and Educational Services.

On preparing for conferences, seminars and meetings

Booth, V. (1993) *Communicating in Science: Writing a Scientific Paper and Speaking at Scientific Meetings*. Cambridge: Cambridge University Press.

Dance, F.E.X. and Zac-Dance, C.C. (1996) *Speaking your Mind: Private Thinking and Public Speaking*, 2nd edn. Dubuque, IA: Kendall/Hunt.

Gosling, P.J. (1999) *Scientist's Guide to Poster Presentations*. New York: Kluwer Publishers.

Mitchell, R.B. (1999) *Tips for Presenting, Chairing, and Discussing at Conferences*, online at http://darkwing.uoregon.edu/~rmitchel/gradprogram/tip_presenting.htm (accessed 20 March 2004).

Presenter's University (2003) http://www.presentersuniversity.com/index.php (accessed 7 January 2004).

Race, P. (1998) *Conference Presentations and Workshops*, online at http://www. phil-race.net/Downloads/Phil's%20conference%20guidelines.doc (accessed, 20 March 2004).

Seekings, D. (1981) *How to Organise Effective Conferences and Meetings*. London: Kogan Page.

Valiela, I. (2001) *Doing Science: Design, Analysis, and Communication of Scientific Research*. Oxford: Oxford University Press.

On being part of a community

Wenger, E. (2000) 'Communities of practice and social learning systems', *Organization*, 7 (2): 225–46.

On the technologies involved in presenting

Application of Presentation Technologies in UK Higher Education (1999) *APT project web site*. http://www2.umist.ac.uk/isd/lwt/apt/home.htm (accessed 15 December 2003).

Mindmanager (2004) *Mindjet's visual tool for brainstorming and planning*, http://www.mindjet.com/uk/index.php (accessed 21 January 2004).

Norvig, P. (2000) *The Gettysburg Powerpoint Presentation*, http://www.norvig.com/ Gettysburg/ (accessed 16 January 2004).

Shephard, K.L. (2003) 'Questioning, promoting and evaluating the use of streaming video to support student learning', *British Journal of Educational Technology*, 34 (3): 297–310.

Wilder, C. and Rotondo, J. (2002) *Point Click and Wow: A Quick Guide to Brilliant Laptop Presentation*. San Francisco, CA: Wiley.

On preparing yourself to give and to receive feedback

Goleman, D. (1997) *Emotional Intelligence*. New York: Bantam Books.

On videoconferencing

BECTA (British Educational Communications and Technology Agency) (2003) 'What the research says about videoconferencing in teaching and learning', http://www.becta.org.uk/page_documents/research/wtrs_vidconf.pdf (accessed 26 November 2003).

Price, D.E. and Spence, A.J. (2003) 'An introduction to H.323 videoconferencing' (Video Technology Advisory Service) http://www.video.ja.net/323intro.pdf (accessed 26 November 2003).

UKERNA (2003) 'UKERNA video conference meetings: how to get the best out of a video conference meeting', http://www.video.ja.net/usrg/U_page4.html (accessed 17 November 2003).

VIDE (2002) *Videoconferencing Cookbook Version 3.0*, http://www.videnet.gatech.edu/cookbook// (accessed 26 November 2003).

On copyright

Nottingham Trent University (2002) *Copyright and Content Development for eLearning*, http://human.ntu.ac.uk/student_staff/resources/elc/copyCont.htm (accessed 12 March 2004).

Shephard, K.L. (2001) 'Submission of student assignments on compact discs: exploring the use of audio, images, and video in assessment and student learning', *British Journal of Educational Technology*, 32 (2): 161–70.

University of Texas *(2004) A crash course in copyright*, http://www.utsystem.edu/ogc/
 intellectualproperty/cprtindx.htm (accessed 12 March 2004).

On evaluation

Assessment-Leeds University Learning and Teaching Pages. http://www.leeds.ac.uk/
 lt/pd.htm (accessed 3 March 2004).
Folding@home. Oral Presentation Rubric. http://www.stanford.edu/group/pandegroup/
 folding/education/rubric.html (accessed 3 March 2004).
Stake, R.E. (1967) 'The countenance of educational evaluation', *Teachers College Record*,
 68 (7): 523–40.

Online video to enliven your presentations

There are many sources of video that can be downloaded or streamed from the Internet.
 Some are copyright free for educational purposes. Some have broader or narrower
 copyright permission.
Online Media Resources (http://www.lib.berkeley.edu/MRC/) (accessed 6 March 2004).
Shephard, K.L. (2003) *Streaming Audio and Video for Course Design*, http://www.
 ltsn.ac.uk (accessed 6 March 2004).

Online images to enliven your presentations

There are now too many sources of good images available on the Internet to list
 individually. Some are copyright free for educational purposes. Some have broader or
 narrower copyright permission. Use Google or another search engine to search for
 images on the topic that interests you. Be careful to avoid finding images that may
 offend you! Images are often not adequately labelled. Sometimes it is only after you
 have seen them that you realize they are not suitable for your presentation, and indeed,
 probably not suitable for you! Images on reputable websites will explain the copyright
 restrictions that apply.

Index